Praise for Sally Pipes and

THE TRUTH ABOUT OBAMACARE

"Sally Pipes shows how a misdiagnosis of the problem led to the wrong pre-scription for American health care. She not only shows what is wrong with the new law, but also puts forward some solid ideas on putting doctors and patients back in charge."

—TOM COBURN, M.D., *Member of Congress*

"Ms. Pipes (a Canadian by birth) established herself as not simply an extraor-dinary expert on health care, but a force of nature, churning out dozens of articles, participating in hundreds of radio and TV interviews, and speaking at countless townhalls across the country. In this new book, she explains why the debate isn't over. Left and right must consider her weighty arguments."

—DAVID GRATZER, M.D. *Senior Fellow, Manhattan Institute*

"Debunking myths, Sally Pipes shows how President Obama and a Democrat Congress have crafted a government takeover of our health care system that will burden families and job creators with new hidden taxes and mandates, increase the deficit, raise health care costs, and impose a government-run bureaucracy between doctors and their patients. The results—lower quality of care, higher costs, and more Washington bureaucrats in charge of our health care decisions. This is a must read for all who want to face the challenges before us."

—TOM PRICE, M.D., *Member of Congress*

"Pipes penetrates the political sloganeering and punctures the wishful think-ing that the anointed 'experts,' long pining for government-managed health care, can deliver universal medical insurance without inflicting unacceptable costs on businesses and individuals and without sacrificing Americans' unique access to valuable health care innovations."

—TOM STOSSEL, M.D., *and Professor of Medicine,*
Harvard Medical School, Massachusetts General Hospital,
and Brigham Women's Hospital

THE
TRUTH ABOUT
OBAMACARE

THE
TRUTH ABOUT
OBAMACARE

SALLY C. PIPES

Since 1947
REGNERY
PUBLISHING, INC.
An Eagle Publishing Company • Washington, DC

Cataloging-in-Publication data on file with the Library of Congress
ISBN 978-1-59698-636-7

Published in the United States by
Regnery Publishing, Inc.
One Massachusetts Avenue, NW
Washington, DC 20001
www.regnery.com

Manufactured in the United States of America
10 9 8 7 6 5 4 3 2 1

Books are available in quantity for promotional or premium use. Write to Director of Special Sales, Regnery Publishing, Inc., One Massachusetts Avenue NW, Washington, DC 20001, for information on discounts and terms or call (202) 216-0600.

Distributed to the trade by:
Perseus Distribution
387 Park Avenue South
New York, NY 10016

To my husband, Charles Kesler, and to Maggie,
whose tolerance for my obsession with
educating Americans on the truth about Obamacare
surpasses all reasonable expectations.

CONTENTS

INTRODUCTION

*After a century of striving, after a year of debate, after a
historic vote, health care reform is no longer an
unmet promise. It is the law of the land.*
—President Barack Obama[1]

On Tuesday, March 23, 2010, surrounded by flashing cameras and cheering fans, Barack Obama signed into law a bill that will lead to the largest expansion of government in the history of the United States.

The president was elated by the bill's passage. White House Senior Advisor David Axelrod admitted that he had "never seen the president so happy about anything—other than his family." Even after winning the presidential election, according to Axelrod, "he was not as excited."[2]

The bill, the Patient Protection and Affordable Care Act, was over 2,400 pages long. Obama used twenty-two commemorative pens to sign it. A week later, he signed a series of amendments that required yet another seventeen pens.[3]

If nothing else, Obamacare is a virtuoso display of regulatory acrobatics. A veritable mountain of parchment, it surely sets a new world record for bureaucratic overkill.

Newspapers say the president's overhaul of our health care system will cost a cool $1 trillion over ten years, give or take a few dollars. But sticker shock is just the beginning.

Make no mistake, Obamacare will crash into our economy and culture with a tidal wave of regulations that, taken together, will fundamentally alter the way we live, work, and access health care.

How will all those changes affect us? That's what this book is about.

WHAT EXACTLY IS OBAMACARE?

For Obama himself, it's clearly the fulfillment of a series of promises made in the midst of a shoot-from-the-hip political campaign. Most of those promises revolved around a general commitment to provide health insurance for all Americans, while lowering costs for individuals and government alike.

Without question, Obama viewed his election victory as a mandate to deliver on those sweeping political promises.

One oft-repeated promise was that, if elected, Obama would reduce the number of uninsured people—which he then put at 45 million[4]—down to zero.

"I will sign a universal health care bill into law by the end of my first term as president that will cover every American," he declared.[5]

He later announced that his plan would "cut the cost of a typical family's premium by up to $2,500 a year."

Moreover, "if you like your current health insurance, nothing changes, except your costs will go down."[6]

But Obama didn't just vow to cover everyone while lowering insurance premiums. He also promised to reduce the government's expenditure on health care. In short, he would use his political muscle to "bend the cost curve," forcing prices down.

Obama promised a minor miracle—a plan that would simultaneously lower the cost of premiums, presumably through government subsidies, while also reducing government outlays.

But Obama didn't stop there. He also assured voters that he'd improve quality. Health care for all would not only cost less, it would be better than what we have today.

"We must redesign our health system to reduce inefficiency and waste and improve health care quality, which will drive down costs for families and individuals."[7]

In one fell swoop, Obama would heal our ailing health care system—cover every single uninsured individual, lower costs for everyone, and improve our quality of care.

Now that's a tall order—some might even call it impossible.

• • •

This book will go over Obamacare with a fine-tooth comb, laying out the specifics of what exists now in the legislation, and where that legislation will likely lead. Most important, we'll look at whether the reality of Obamacare measures up to the promise.

We'll look at Obamacare's attempts to reduce the ranks of the uninsured by simply forcing Americans to purchase insurance. Those who refuse will be fined.

Businesses will also be coerced into providing insurance to their employees—and will be fined if they don't.

Medicare and Medicare Advantage—which provide coverage to senior citizens—will be cut.

Meanwhile, Medicaid will be dramatically expanded to cover 18 million of the additional 34 million people who will now be insured. One of the most financially unstable and ineffective programs of our government, Medicaid is already detested by doctors and patients alike. Now it will grow exponentially.[8]

On top of that, childless adults will now be eligible for taxpayer-subsidized coverage that was originally set up to help impoverished children.

We'll look at the many frightening ways in which Obamacare will attempt to lower costs—often by depriving people of top-quality medical care.

For example, the new law will impose "comparative effectiveness research" upon the country—laying the groundwork for a system in which bureaucrats can deny coverge of cutting-edge medicines in order to save the government money.

Obamacare will also massively increase regulation of the insurance market. The government will dictate to insurance companies what they must include in their coverage—from addiction care to prosthetics to fertility treatments—and how much they must spend on claims.

• • •

These changes and their myriad offshoots will require a huge new bureaucracy of administrators, regulators, consultants, and experts dedicated to enforcing compliance, penalizing taxpayers, hounding insurance companies, and making all this happen at a supposedly lower cost.

Out of the gate, the legislation sets up an astounding 159 new boards and commissions.

There's an Elder Justice Coordinating Council, a Pregnancy Assistance Fund, and an Office of Indian Men's Health. And the list goes on and on.

How will Obamacare be enforced?

For starters, 16,000 new IRS agents will be hired to track down individuals and businesses that don't purchase insurance, offer insurance, or fill out the required reams of forms.

Those IRS agents will also collect Obamacare's new taxes.

Starting in 2013, individuals with incomes over $200,000 a year and families making more than $250,000 will see their Medicare payroll taxes increase.

Moreover, many will find themselves subject to a brand new tax—a whopping 3.8 percent Medicare tax set to fall on unearned income—interest, rental income, capital gains, and dividend income.

Also, the bill halves the amount of money people can set aside in Flexible Spending Accounts for routine medical expenses. And people who face catastrophic health care expenses in a given year will find their allowable tax deductions considerably diminished. There will be a host of new regulations on how people can use Health Savings Accounts.

● ● ●

Obamacare will transfer one-sixth of our economy into the hands of politicians and agency bureaucrats—leading us down the road to a single-payer, "Medicare for All" system that virtually guarantees a spectacular failure.

Not even other government agencies predict success. By 2019, 23 million people will remain uninsured, according to the Congressional Budget Office.[9] Even worse, Obamacare won't reduce costs at all. In fact, it will drive the country's health care bill ever higher, according to economic experts at the Health and Human Services Department.[10]

After Obamacare passed, the president declared that his campaign promise to reform the system "was finally fulfilled."[11]

We'll see about that.

CHAPTER 1

A GLIMPSE INTO THE FUTURE

n February 2010, Danny Williams, the premier of the Canadian province of Newfoundland, traveled to the United States to undergo heart valve surgery at Mount Sinai hospital in Miami, Florida. He wanted to see a specialist with expertise in minimally invasive heart operations. He paid out of his own pocket for the procedure. When the Canadian media asked Williams questions about it, he said, "This was my heart, my choice, and my health."[1]

Williams's story isn't unique. With his trip, he joined a long list of high-ranking Canadians who have decided that, when their lives are on the line, they prefer American medicine to their own country's government-run health system.

In June 2007, former Liberal Member of Parliament Belinda Stronach traveled to California for a late-stage breast cancer operation—even though, while in office, she had opposed any privatization of Canadian health care. Late Quebec Premier Robert Bourassa went south too, for skin cancer treatment.

Meanwhile, tens of thousands of ordinary Canadians head to the United States every year to spend their savings on critical medical care.

It's not just America's next-door neighbors who are doing it. Thousands of other foreigners, many of them Europeans, visit the United States each year for treatment. Among the most prominent was Italian Prime Minister Silvio Berlusconi, who traveled to the Cleveland Clinic in late 2006 for heart surgery, foregoing the supposedly glorious free health care he could have received in Italy.

It doesn't make the news when less-prominent Europeans come, but plenty do. Usually they need advanced procedures that are either unavailable in their own countries or rationed under universal health care systems.

Foreigners also come to get the newest drugs. Government-run systems, trying to keep costs under control, often decline to provide cutting-edge medicines when they first become available. Many Canadians drive south of the border to get drugs like Glucophage XR, which treats type 2 diabetes, and Rituxan, a cancer treatment. (Rituxan has now been approved in some Canadian provinces.)[2]

OBAMA'S END GAME

When he was running for president, Obama made it clear that his goal was a system of universal health care.

In May 2007, he told an audience of union workers, "We can have universal health care by the end of the next president's first term, by the end of my first term."[3]

A couple weeks later, at a speech in Iowa City, he declared that "the time has come for universal, affordable health care in America."[4]

While Obama acknowledged that a single-payer system—a system where all medical costs and payments are run through the government—might be impractical to implement, he made it clear that if he were starting with a blank slate, that's what he would endorse. "If I were designing a system from scratch I would probably set up a single-payer system," he said in Iowa in 2007.[5]

In the health care bill that was passed in March 2010, Obama didn't achieve his dream, but his objective is clear, and he did manage to move the system in the direction he wants to go—closer to the systems in Canada and Europe. Let's take a closer look at those systems, because they give us a glimpse into the future.

THE MYTH OF FREE CARE

Proponents of universal care often claim that health care in places like Canada is "free."

That's inaccurate.

No matter who pays up front, goods and services remain costly to produce. Doctors, nurses, and hospital staffers cost money. So do drugs, MRI machines, and latex gloves. Universal health care doesn't suddenly make health care free; it centralizes it in the hands of one giant institution, the government.

A giant institution providing a service for tens of millions of people has to do certain things to survive. If a centralized system paid for everything patients ever wanted, costs would quickly spiral out of control. To prevent that from happening, governments have to ration services and drugs. In a free market, patients can buy the services they need, when they need them. Under a centralized system, patients have to get on waiting lists for common procedures because governments simply can't afford to provide all citizens with the care they need when they need it.

In Canada, for example, 694,161 people were on waiting lists for surgery and other necessary treatments in 2009. That same year, the average wait between a referral by a general practitioner and treatment by a specialist was 16.1 weeks.[6] That's 73 percent longer than it was in 1993[7], and almost double what most doctors consider acceptable.

ANTIQUATED MEDICAL EQUIPMENT

Once a Canadian patient finally makes it into the examination or operating room, there's a good chance that his doctor is using antiquated equipment. The country's health care system employs far too many old and potentially unreliable medical technologies. Many machines should have been junked years ago. Others will need to be replaced in the near future.

Doctors are using the old technologies because the wait for many new ones—including CT (computed tomography) scans, MRI (magnetic resonance imaging) scans, and ultrasound scans—is just too long. In 2009, the median national wait for a CT scan was 4.6 weeks.[8]

According to the Fraser Institute, the European Coordination Committee of the Radiological and Electromedical Industries (ECCREI) recommends that no more than 10 percent of a country's health technology inventory be older than ten years. Beyond that age, the equipment is not considered state-of-the-art and thus could pose a health hazard or lead to substandard treatment of patients.

The Canadian health system doesn't even come close to adhering to this standard. As of 2007, the share of its medical inventory that's over a decade old includes 21 percent of its bone densitometers, which are used to measure the bone density of osteoporosis patients, and 28 percent of its SPECT units, which are used to create three-dimensional images of the body.

A third of Canada's gamma cameras, which are used in nuclear medicine imaging, and a quarter of its angiography and cardiac catheterization labs for heart-related ailments, are more than ten years old. Canada has comparatively few lithotripters to fight kidney and gall stones, and a third of the machines are more than a decade old.

The ECCREI also recommends that 60 percent of a country's medical machines be less than five years old. Canada's hospital inventories fail in this regard for a seemingly endless list of different machines: bone densitometers, MRI machines, SPECT units, gamma cameras, lithotripters, and angiography suites, to name a few.

The widespread use of antiquated medical equipment puts Canada's patient population in a dangerous position. These machines are liable to break down during treatment. Older imaging technologies may yield low-quality images, which can cause doctors to misdiagnose conditions and prescribe ineffective or even harmful treatments.

WHERE ARE THE DOCTORS?

Another reason for long waits to see specialists in Canada is that Canada has a shortage of doctors.

Canada ranks twenty-sixth out of thirty countries for number of doctors per thousand people, according to the Organization for Economic Cooperation and Development.[9] That ranking has fallen steadily since 1970, when the government took over the health care system. Back then, Canada ranked fourth.[10]

One reason for the physician shortage is that over the last ten years, some 11 percent of doctors trained in Canadian medical schools have moved to the United States. That's because the average Canadian doctor, paid by the provincial government, earns only 42 percent of what an American doctor earns. This has led to a brain drain.

FARTHER AFIELD

Canada's problems are typical of all universal health care systems. Over the last few years, we've seen countless sad stories of European patients unable to get the care they need.

In 2009, British newspapers reported the story of Ian Boynton, a former soldier who was forced to pull out thirteen of his own teeth with a pair of pliers after thirty failed attempts to find a dentist through the country's National Health Service (NHS).[11]

Horror stories like this are common in Britain. Right now, a shortage of hospital beds and midwives is forcing thousands of mothers to give birth in hospital hallways, bathrooms, and even elevators. In 2008 alone, there were 4,000 cases of expectant mothers in British hospitals having to give birth in places other than a maternity ward.[12]

Believe it or not, these mothers were fortunate to have been seen by a doctor at all. Every year, Britain's National Health Service (NHS) cancels around 100,000 operations.[13] As of 2008, more than one million Britons were waiting for hospital admission.[14]

Meanwhile, many British hospitals are in disrepair. Each year more than 100,000 patients contract infections or illnesses that they didn't have before being admitted to NHS hospitals.[15]

The story is the same under the government health care system in France, which is regularly stretched to its limits, and in Sweden. There, some patients stuck on waiting lists have resorted to going to veterinarians, who operate in the private market and are in plentiful supply.[16] Many Swedes go to neighboring countries for dental care, even though they've paid taxes for the service at home.

THE TRUTH ABOUT "CHEAPER" DRUGS

Some in the United States have advanced the argument that prescription drugs are cheaper overseas, and argued that a universal health care system could do better than what Americans have at home. It's true, for instance, that some drugs in Britain sell for less than they do in the United States, but that's because the government imposes price controls. The downside is that because the prices are kept artificially low (and taxpayers pay to keep them low) supplies are limited, and many British patients are denied access to the newest lifesaving medicines because the NHS considers them unnecessary.

Britain has a government agency whose job it is to limit people's access to drugs. The National Institute for Health and Clinical Effectiveness (NICE) determines which treatments the NHS should cover.

Back in 2001, when Americans with leukemia were welcoming the arrival of the miracle drug Gleevec, NICE concluded that Gleevec wasn't any more effective against leukemia than existing medicines. It was two years before the British government changed its mind.[17]

Then in 2002, Americans with a rare stomach cancer started taking Gleevec because it was found to target and kill cancer cells without attacking healthy cells. It took almost another two years after U.S. approval for Britain to approve using Gleevec for the same rare cancer.[18]

In early 2008, the NHS refused to approve abatacept, an arthritis drug that is sold in the United States under the brand-name Orencia. Even though abatacept is one of the only drugs proven to improve severe rheumatoid arthritis, NICE determined that "abatacept would not be a cost-effective use of NHS resources."[19]

Even when the NHS approves drugs eventually, the lost time between the availability of a drug in the marketplace and access for British patients endangers lives. Consider the lung cancer drug Tarceva.

By 2005, Tarceva was being used throughout Europe.[20] Yet NICE determined that the drug was too expensive to cover, despite numerous peer-reviewed studies showing that the drug was significantly prolonging the life of cancer patients.[21]

Patient groups grew incensed, and the Roy Castle Foundation—Britain's largest lung cancer charity—urged NICE to reverse its decision. But it didn't matter—NICE continued to drag its feet. By 2008, Britain was one of just three countries in Western Europe where Tarceva wasn't covered. Finally, in November 2008, the NHS began paying for the drug.[22]

Who knows how many lives could have been saved if only the NHS had approved Tarceva immediately?

WHERE THE UNITED STATES EXCELS

Despite all the problems of rationing, American proponents of universal care have repeatedly held up foreign systems as superior. But by the most important measure—serving those who are sick—the United States excels.

The United States is the world leader, for instance, in treating cancer. A 2008 study in *Lancet Oncology* found that, compared to Europeans and Canadians, Americans have a better survival rate—five years after diagnoses—for thirteen out of sixteen of the most common cancers.[23]

Consider breast cancer. The survival rate among American women is 83.9 percent, while in Britain it's just 69.7 percent.

For men with prostate cancer, the survival rate is 91.9 percent in the United States, 73.7 percent in France, and 51.1 percent in Britain.

American men and women are more than 35 percent more likely to survive colon cancer than British citizens.[24]

Meanwhile, many of the statistics used to portray the United States as having poor medical outcomes are derived by manipulating the data—essentially comparing apples to oranges.

Life expectancy in the United States reached 77.9 in 2007, according to the Centers for Disease Control and Prevention.[25] That represents a steady increase, but it still puts the United States behind about thirty other countries. In Sweden, France, Canada, Japan, and Hong Kong, life expectancy is well beyond 80.

But wait. Indicators like life expectancy and infant mortality reflect a variety of factors, and medical care is just one of them. Life expectancy is also affected by a country's homicide rate, the number of accidents, diet trends, ethnic diversity, and so on.

The United States, sadly, has a higher homicide rate than many other Western nations. In 2004 the rate was 5.9 per 100,000 inhabitants.[26] In contrast, the rate was 1.95 in Canada, 1.64 in France, and .98 in Germany.[27]

The United States also has more car accidents. The Department of Transportation estimates that there were 14.24 fatalities per 100,000 people from auto accidents in 2006.[28] In

Canada, the number was 9.25, in France, 7.4, and in Germany, just 6.19.[29]

Homicides and car accidents alone significantly bring down life expectancy. Not surprisingly, Robert Ohsfeldt of Texas A&M and John Schneider of the University of Iowa recently found that Americans who don't die in homicides or car accidents outlive people in every other Western country.[30]

As Harvard economist Greg Mankiw has noted, "These differences have lessons for traffic laws and gun control, but they teach us nothing about our system of health care."[31]

Likewise, the U.S. health care system is often criticized for having an infant mortality rate that's higher than the rates in Europe. But does America's infant mortality really signify that its health care system is inferior? The evidence suggests the facts are being manipulated.

The World Health Organization (WHO) defines a live birth as any infant that, once removed from its mother, "breathes or shows any other evidence of life such as beating of the heart, pulsation of the umbilical cord, or definite movement of voluntary muscles."[32] The United States follows that definition, counting all births that show any sign of life, regardless of birth weight or prematurity.

Other nations, however, use a different standard. In France, authorities require a "medical certificate stating that the child was born alive and viable" in order to attest the death of a baby.[33]

In Switzerland, "an infant must be at least 30 centimeters long at birth to be counted as living."[34]

In France and Belgium, babies born at less than twenty-six weeks are simply registered as dead.[35]

With fewer babies declared to be alive, fewer are counted as having passed away.

In fact, when our Canadian neighbors have extremely high-risk births, they're often rushed to the United States for the delivery. An August 2007 story in the *Calgary Herald* sums it up nicely:

> A rare set of identical quadruplets, born...to a Calgary woman at a Montana hospital, are in good health....The naturally conceived baby quads—Autumn, Brooke, Calissa, and Dahlia were delivered by caesarean section Sunday in Great Falls....Their mother, Calgarian Karen Jepp, was transferred to Benefis Hospital in Montana last week when she began showing signs of going into labour, and no Canadian hospital had enough neonatal intensive-care beds for all four babies.[36]

There's another way in which we should also be careful about accepting statistics at face value. One of the most widely quoted international sources during the health care debate was the WHO's *World Health Report 2000*. It ranked the United States 37th out of 191 countries in overall health system performance. Yet, though we have seen that life expectancy is at best a crude measure, WHO used that factor alone to account for a full 25 percent of how a nation's health care system was ranked.[37]

Another 25 percent of the ranking came from "distribution of health," or fairness.[38] But by that reasoning, treating everyone exactly the same is more important, as a measure of health, than treating people well. A nation where everyone was poorly but equally treated would do well in the WHO ranking.

TURNING TO A FREER MARKET

Ironically, even as the United States is expanding the role of government in health care, many Canadian and European leaders are pushing for just the opposite. They've tried socialized medicine and seen the costs. The United States doesn't have to go and make the same mistakes—though that seems to be what the Obama administration wants.

Consider the story of Claude Castonguay. In 1966, the premier of the province of Quebec asked Castonguay to head a commission on health reform. He recommended that Quebec adopt a system of public health insurance. The Quebec government followed his advice, and soon, other Canadian provinces followed suit. Castonguay became known as the father of Quebec medicare.[39]

In March 2007, as the cost of health care in Quebec spiraled out of control and waiting lists lengthened, the government of Quebec again asked Castonguay to lead a task force. This time he was charged with looking into new ways to finance the health care system.[40] Castonguay concluded that it was in "crisis," and called on the private sector to play a greater role.

Shortly before that, in 2005, the Supreme Court of Canada struck down a Quebec law banning private medical insurance.

According to the court, since patients often had to wait months to see a doctor, opting out of the public system and buying private insurance was often the only way to receive treatment in a timely manner.

As Madam Chief Justice Beverley McLachlin put it in her majority ruling, "Access to a waiting list is not access to health care."[41]

Upon taking office last year, Dr. Anne Doig, the Canadian Medical Association president, characterized Canada's socialized health care system as "sick" and "imploding."[42] Elsewhere, too, lawmakers are realizing that without unlimited funding, it's impossible to dole out enough health care services to meet demand.

Since the end of World War II, the private sector has played a small role in the British health system. Most people have always gone through the NHS. Meanwhile those with enough money either bought their own insurance, or paid cash to doctors to jump the queue when they needed treatment. Increasingly, though, the government is looking toward private-sector providers to help save a broken system.[43]

In the 1990s, under the "private finance initiative," private sector companies began building hospitals.[44] Today British health care would be in even worse shape if it weren't being increasingly assisted by the private sector.

THE LAST BEST HOPE

The United States is certainly in need of health care reform. Unfortunately, Obamacare takes the country in an entirely wrong direction, toward the universal systems that have already been tried, with poor results, in Canada and Europe.

That's bad news for the United States, and also for the rest of the world, because when people look for high quality health care, they look to the United States.

Whereas other nations rarely invent new drugs, the United States, with its free market system, has continued to innovate and come up with new medicines. When national health care systems have failed, unable to provide the diagnoses and treatments people need, their citizens have been able to come to the United States.

Now the United States is turning to a system that will ration medicine, close hospitals, and drive doctors out of business.

Twenty years down the road, where will people like Newfoundland premier Danny Williams—and the rest of us—turn for top-notch medical care?

CHAPTER 2

HOW U.S. HEALTH CARE BECAME DISABLED

When it comes to reforming health care, everyone can agree that our goal should be affordable, accessible, high quality health care for all—but Obamacare takes us in the wrong direction.

For all its virtues, the American health care system was in need of reform before Obamacare. In 2009, our country spent 17.3 percent of our gross domestic product (GDP), or $2.5 trillion, on health care,[1] the highest rate in the world. Tens of millions of Americans are uninsured,[2] often because insurance is too expensive. Americans who do have health insurance, meanwhile, are often frustrated because of the restrictions of managed care. Although Obamacare posed as the answer to these problems, it will make most of them worse.

HOW DID WE GET HERE?

To understand how U.S. health care got to be such a mess, we have to go back to the 1940s. During World War II, President Franklin D. Roosevelt's administration imposed wage and price controls in an effort to help finance the war,

Companies competing to hire workers at government-controlled wages looked for ways to offer extras. Health benefits turned out to be very popular,[3] and employers adopted the habit of not reporting the value of the benefits to the IRS as wages.

On October 26, 1943, the IRS issued a tax ruling confirming that health benefits paid by employers were tax exempt. Canadian physician and health care policy expert David Gratzer has called that ruling "the biggest event to shape American health insurance."

The effect was to formalize a system of third-party payments.

We purchase most goods and services directly from the producer. In health care, however, it became normal for someone else to pay—either an insurance company, an employer, or, eventually, a government-run body like Medicare. Countries with universal health care, like Canada, also use a third-party system, only it's the government rather than an insurance company that pays the bills.

In both cases, the result is rationing. No large organization with a fixed budget can provide everything everyone wants all the time, so they impose limits on who can get what and when. The results are, inevitably, waiting lists, restrictions on doctor visits, and lack of access to some treatments or drugs.

America's third-party system doesn't simply distort the free market. It's also deeply unfair. People working for large corporations receive health insurance that their employers purchase for them with pre-tax dollars; while those who work for themselves must pay for health insurance with their own after-tax income. This tax policy punishes entrepreneurs, the self-employed, and anyone else who doesn't work for a company that provides health insurance.

THE EXPANSION OF GOVERNMENT

The federal government's unfair tax rule was just the beginning of a massive intrusion into the health care marketplace. In 1946, President Harry Truman signed the Hospital Survey and Construction Act, which pumped $4.6 billion of federal taxpayer money into building non-profit hospitals. In exchange for a federal subsidy, the hospitals had to provide charity care for the poor.[4]

In 1965, the government enacted Medicare to provide health care for the elderly, and Medicaid to do the same for the poor. These two programs substantially expanded the third-party system and the role of the federal government in health care.

The reforms that took place from the 1940s through the 1960s didn't bring about the accessible, affordable, high-quality care everyone wanted. In fact, as the science of medicine progressed rapidly, America's system for delivering medicine got worse. In 1969, President Richard Nixon said, "We face a crisis in this area."[5]

As is always the case with government programs, politicians kept pressing for an even bigger Washington role. The National Governors' Conference endorsed a resolution calling for national health insurance, while the Senate Finance Committee considered a government takeover of catastrophic insurance.[6]

In 1971, Nixon unveiled a new national health care strategy. In it, he endorsed health maintenance organizations (HMOs), which he thought could keep costs down. He wanted nearly everyone (90 percent of the people) to have the option of enrolling in an HMO within ten years.[7] Nixon's HMO plan, the Health Maintenance Act of 1973, passed with bipartisan support.

The new law included a mix of regulations to dramatically increase the use of HMOs. It mandated that companies with more than twenty-five workers offer employees at least one HMO as an option.[8] And it included $1.6 billion[9] in grants and loans for businesses that wanted to start HMOs.[10]

Eventually, HMOs went mainstream. They did keep costs under control—but their aggressive cost-cutting became so unpopular[11] that by the early 2000s, politicians campaigned against them.

RECENT "REFORMS"

In 1992, Bill Clinton touted himself as the health care reform candidate. As president, he appointed First Lady Hillary Clinton to lead a health care task force that would create a universal health care plan.

Hillarycare demanded that all Americans buy health insurance, mandated that employers provide HMO plans to their workers, and imposed additional restrictions and regulations on insurance providers. The plan proved to be so unpopular that it met with a bipartisan defeat in Congress.

But Clinton did get one health care reform passed. In 1997 the State Children's Health Insurance Program, or SCHIP, was established with the best of intentions—to provide health insurance to low-income children in households that didn't qualify for Medicaid.

By the time it was up for reauthorization ten years later, SCHIP covered about 6.6 million children.[12] But thanks to a flaw in the program's funding formula, coverage expanded well beyond the intended recipients.

By 2007 only 83 percent of those enrolled were children in the target income group. The rest were adults and children above the income threshold.[13] When Democrats reauthorized SCHIP for the second time in 2009, they added $32.8 billion in spending to expand coverage even more.

WHERE WILL IT END?

Through all these reform efforts, health care costs have spiraled upwards. As Milton Friedman observed, "As a fraction of national income, spending on medical care went from 3 percent of the national income in 1919 to 4.5 percent in 1946 to 7 percent in 1965 to a mind-boggling 17 percent in 1997."[14] Despite all this, the expansion of the government's role in health care has continued, right up to the passage of the Obama health care bill in 2010.

Clearly, America's health care system has many problems. But to fix them, we first need to recognize that they were created by government policies that drove a third-party wedge between consumers and insurance companies and distorted the insurance market. Obamacare adds to the problem by ensuring that the government will play an even bigger role in the health insurance industry in years to come. According to the Centers for Medicare and Medicaid Services, the government will be responsible for 52 percent of the nation's health care spending by 2019.[15] Any attempt to fix our health care system by pouring in more tax dollars for more government programs that employ more government bureaucrats is, to put it plainly, unlikely to succeed. If we want efficiency, low costs, and high quality service, we need to let the market do its work.

CHAPTER 3

HISTORY OF OBAMACARE

n the 2008 presidential primaries, Democrat contenders Hillary Clinton and Barack Obama both promised universal health care. They said their plans would achieve lower overall health care costs without imposing new taxes on the middle class.

The key difference in their plans, Obama said repeatedly, was that he was against any mandate that would force individuals to purchase insurance. (Once president, of course, he completely reversed his position.)

At a dinner in Virginia on February 9, 2008, he said, "The one difference between my plan and Senator Clinton's plan is that she said she'd 'go after' your wages if you don't buy health care. Well I believe the reason people don't have health care isn't because no one's forced them to buy it, it's because no one's made it affordable."[1]

A few weeks later, during the February 21 presidential debate, Obama again criticized Clinton for her mandate proposal and denounced the individual mandate that had been imposed in Massachusetts.

"They have exempted 20 percent of the uninsured because they've concluded that 20 percent can't afford it. In some cases, there are people who are paying fines and still can't afford it so now they're worse off than they were. They don't have health insurance and they're paying a fine. In order for you to force people to get health insurance, you've got to have a very harsh, stiff penalty, and Senator Clinton has said that we will go after their wages."[2]

Obama called his anti-mandate stance a "substantive difference" between his proposal and Clinton's.

A DEMOCRATIC OBSESSION

As president, Obama made health care reform his most important domestic policy issue.

Unlike President Clinton, who attempted to craft a health care reform package in the executive branch, President Obama wanted the reform to be developed in the House and Senate.

Early drafts included a government health insurance plan or "public option" as an alternative to private insurance,[3] and a mandate that individuals buy insurance. Later, there were debates about adding a subsidy for low-income families to help them buy insurance. By August, public opposition to the bill had grown so strong that Democrats were struggling to maintain support for it within their own ranks.[4]

IS ANYBODY LISTENING?

In early 2009, popular opposition to the Democrats' health care reform helped fuel the anti-big-government Tea Party movement. Polls suggested that independents, who had swung Obama's way in the 2008 election, were abandoning him in large numbers because they didn't like his big government agenda.[5]

By January 19, 2010, a national NBC/*Wall Street Journal* poll found that only 33 percent of the American people thought the health care bill was a good idea, while 46 percent thought it was a bad idea.[6]

In the November 3, 2009, gubernatorial races, two Democrat governors were replaced by Republicans: New Jersey residents elected Chris Christie with 48.8 percent of the vote, and Virginians elected Bob McDonnell with 58.6 percent. Neither candidate supported the Democrats' health care reform.

Ironically, as popular support for health care reform collapsed, big business lobbies—the same ones so many Democrats vilify—rallied behind it.

The drug lobby (the Pharmaceutical Research and Manufacturers of America, or PhRMA) hailed Obama's health care reform as "important and historic." PhRMA spent more than $26 million lobbying in 2009 as the bill was taking shape, the most expensive campaign by any industry lobby ever.[7]

The Democratic reform efforts were also supported by corporate giant General Electric, the AARP, the American Medical Association (which represents only 17 percent of doctors in the United States), and the American Hospital Association, which is the fifth-biggest industry lobby.

Strange, then, that in December 2009, Obama described the Senate vote for the bill as "standing up to the special interests."[8]

The drug lobby could have written elements of the final bill: it requires employers to give workers prescription drug coverage, requires states to subsidize drugs through Medicaid, and prohibits Americans from importing cheaper drugs from China, among other provisions.[9]

Meanwhile, transparency was cast to the wayside. Starting in August 2009, all congressional recesses were cancelled, keeping politicians away from their constituents.

In the halls of Congress, doors were locked while health care negotiations took place. And when Pelosi announced the unveiling of the House bill, she held a rally on the steps of the Capitol—but it wasn't open to the public. Chain-link fences surrounded the normally open West Front of the Capitol to control access.[10]

DEMOCRATS' NEW MATH

Originally, the president assured Americans that health-reform legislation would mean lower health care costs.

The House bill presented for a vote in November, though, suggested higher costs,[11] according to an analysis by the Congressional Budget Office (CBO), the nonpartisan government agency that provides economic information to Congress.

According to an estimate by Richard S. Foster, the chief actuary for the Centers for Medicare and Medicaid Services, one version of the bill would have driven health spending 2.1 percent higher than it would otherwise been over ten years.[12]

Although Democratic House leaders made it a goal to get the cost of the bill under $900 billion over ten years, they managed to do so only by using some very strange accounting.

The House bill, for instance, proposed to start collecting new and higher taxes to pay for health care in 2010. But coverage and benefits weren't slated to start until 2014 or later.[13]

As health care reporter Robert Pear wrote in the *New York Times*, "By the most commonly used yardstick, the bill would cost $1.05 trillion over ten years, roughly $150 billion more than President Obama had said he wanted to spend on the legislation."[14]

Even using accounting tricks to whittle the total down to $900 billion, the tally still didn't include the so-called "Doc Fix" (which was restoring $245 billion dollars in payments to doctors from Medicare that was originally slated to be cut). To hide this additional cost, House Speaker Nancy Pelosi introduced it in an entirely separate bill.[15]

On November 7, 2009, the House narrowly approved its version of health care reform legislation by 220 votes to 215. This bill was called the Affordable Health Care for America Act. Only one Republican voted for it, and only thirty-nine Democrats opposed it.[16]

THE SENATE VERSION

The Senate, meanwhile, moved forward with its own bill. But even with a Democratic supermajority, passage wasn't easy, as several Democrats were on the fence.

Nebraska Senator Ben Nelson threatened to filibuster the bill, until senators amended it to include higher rates of Medicaid reimbursements for Nebraska. Pundits nicknamed this amendment the "cornhusker kickback," and Nelson turned around to support the bill.

Democrats also won the support of Senator Mary Landrieu of Louisiana through the "Louisiana purchase," the nickname given to a provision that gives extra Medicaid funding to any state in which every county has been declared a disaster area. At the time, only Louisiana, affected by Hurricane Katrina, qualified.[17]

On December 24, with the support of Nelson and Landrieu, the Senate voted 60 to 39 along party lines to pass their bill. Obama's promises that health care reform would be bipartisan were by now dead. Every single Democrat backed the bill. Not a single Republican—not even Maine's Olympia Snowe, who had spoken many times in support of health care reform—voted in favor.[18]

SCOTT BROWN'S UPSET VICTORY

Democrats were confident, but the game was by no means over, as the differences between the House and Senate bills now needed to be straightened out in conference. Then, on January 19, 2010, before the reconciliation of the House and Senate bills, Republican Scott Brown pulled off a stunning (and hugely embarrassing, for the Democrats) victory in the special election to fill the United States Senate seat formerly held by Ted Kennedy in Massachusetts. That meant the Democrats no longer had a supermajority in the Senate.

Not only was this one of the great upsets in modern political history, but it was a telling one for the Democrats' health care bill. Massachusetts was the only state that had implemented a health care plan along the same lines as the one proposed in the national reform bill; so the election turned into a referendum on Obamacare.

Did Massachusetts voters think the country should follow in the footsteps of the Bay State's health reforms?

The answer was a resounding "no."

Brown's surprise win suddenly gave Republicans enough seats to filibuster the bill. To make matters worse for the Democrats, the majority of Americans now clearly opposed their legislation.[19]

THE END GAME

Some blue dog Democrats began getting nervous about supporting the health care bill, so the Democrat leadership played hardball in earnest. In January, Democrat leaders agreed to reconcile the House and Senate bills behind closed doors,[20] all the better to twist arms.

Rather than risk allowing dueling House and Senate bills to delay passage, Nancy Pelosi urged her caucus to abandon the House version of the bill and pass the Senate version instead. As she did so, she orchestrated amendments to appease various members of her constituency, and thus secure enough votes for passage.[21]

But these amendments couldn't be added directly to the Senate version of the bill. They would need to be passed as an entirely separate bill using a controversial legislative process known as reconciliation.

Pelosi was desperate to pass something immediately—and she pushed hard. Her members didn't even have time to read the Senate legislation. On March 9, 2010, she commented, "We have to pass the bill so that you can find out what is in it."[22] That was hardly reassuring, given that the final Senate bill was more than 2,400 pages long.[23]

While Pelosi worked Congress, White House Chief of Staff Rahm Emanuel worked behind the scenes.

Bart Stupak, the Michigan anti-abortion Democrat, was leading a small faction of Democrats who had been withholding support for the bill for fear that federal funding would go to providing abortions.

Late in March 2010, Stupak said Emanuel approached him in the House gym and offered a compromise, namely that Obama would issue an executive order clarifying the ban on federal funding for abortion. Stupak and six other House members accepted the offer and came on board.[24]

Pelosi now had the votes she needed for the House to pass the Senate version of the health care reform bill. It was passed by the House on March 21, 2010.

CONTROVERSIAL RECONCILIATION

The House then sent its amendments to the Senate. This third bill was called the Health Care and Education Reconciliation Act of 2010.

The Senate passed this third bill using the controversial "reconciliation" process, which allowed Democrats to avoid a Republican filibuster.

Congress had never before used reconciliation to pass a major policy change. The arcane procedure, first deployed in 1980,[25] was typically used only to fast-track legislation affecting budgets and the deficit. The rules for using reconciliation required that everything in the bill have an impact on federal spending. Debate is limited, and, instead of requiring the usual sixty votes, the bill can pass with only fifty-one.

In the past, Democrat and Republican lawmakers alike resisted using reconciliation except on budget-focused bills with bipartisan support.

In fact, it was Democratic West Virginia Senator Robert C. Byrd who once led the charge to restrict the use of reconciliation, creating the "Byrd rule" that allows the Senate parliamentarian to strip any items in the bill deemed "extraneous." Byrd was also among the Democratic leaders who urged President Bill Clinton not to use the reconciliation process to push through his health care agenda.[26]

Though reconciliation was clearly not intended for passing laws as complicated and contentious as the health care bill, that's how Democrats used it.

In the final days before passage, the majority of Americans clearly opposed the bill.[27] A CNN poll conducted from March 19 to 20 found that 59 percent opposed the legislation while only 39 percent supported it.[28] A survey by Rasmussen Reports just before the vote found that 54 percent opposed the bill and

41 percent supported it. Just after passage of the bill, a *Washington Post* survey found that 50 percent of Americans opposed the bill, and that 46 percent supported it.[29]

With anemic support from the American people, the president signed the Patient Protection and Affordable Care Act into law on March 23, 2010.

THE AFTERMATH

Almost as soon as the bill passed, new estimates of its impact started rolling in. In April 2010, Richard S. Foster—the chief actuary of the Centers for Medicare & Medicaid Services—released a detailed examination of the new law.[30]

Foster found that overall health spending under the health reform act would in fact be $311 billion higher from 2010 to 2019 than it otherwise would have been.[31] He also found that 23 million people would still be uninsured by 2019.

The Congressional Budget Office released a report predicting that nearly 4 million Americans would have to pay the new penalty for not getting health insurance, with penalties averaging about $1,000 apiece in 2016.[32] The penalties will begin in 2014.

And that was just the beginning. The biggest expansion of health care coverage since 1965, Obamacare restructures nearly 20 percent of America's economy.[33] Its shockwaves will be reverberating for years.

CHAPTER 4

DISSECTING
THE LEGISLATION

What's in the Obamacare bill? Plenty. The bill itself is 2,409 pages, to which 153 pages were added to iron out kinks in the Senate bill. These 2,562 pages are almost exactly double the length of Vintage Classics' 1,296-page edition of *War and Peace*.

At least Leo Tolstoy offered his readers a plot. Rather than a clear narrative, Obamacare features a dizzying array of rapidly moving parts. Some whirl clockwise, others twirl counterclockwise, and even more leap up and down like pogo sticks.

Obamacare is to be implemented in phases from 2010 to 2020. Generally speaking, it collects taxes early and offers benefits late. If Obamacare survives the legal challenges it faces (including lawsuits from at least twenty state attorneys general seeking to block it),[1] how will it look once fully implemented?

BUY HEALTH INSURANCE...OR ELSE

At the heart of Obamacare is the mandate that nearly every American citizen and legal resident carry health insurance. This is the first time Congress has required Americans to buy something. It's also a policy Obama campaigned against while running for president in 2008.

Those who ignore this mandate will pay a price. By 2016, non-compliance will cost individuals $695, or 2.5 percent of household income up to $2,085, whichever is higher.[2]

As Republican Congressman Steve King of Iowa observed, "The recently passed Obamacare legislation authorizes as much as $10 billion dollars for the IRS and will enable the IRS to hire 16,000 to 17,000 new agents to force compliance."[3]

These new agents will ensure that Americans obey these new rules. On the bright side, Congress is creating jobs—and at Washington, D.C.'s most beloved address, no less.

IRS officials concede that Obamacare does not empower the agency to tap the bank accounts or prosecute those who defy the individual mandate. However, "There are tools we can use," IRS Deputy Commissioner Steven T. Miller told the Senate Finance Committee—on tax day, April 15, fittingly enough. Evidently, the IRS plans to reduce or eliminate tax refunds for those who refuse to buy health insurance.[4]

Reportedly exempted from the mandate to own health insurance—and therefore safe from having their tax refunds impounded—are some religious groups, such as Christian Scientists, who are uncomfortable with modern medicine, as well as Scientologists, whose criticisms are less clear, and Muslims who might oppose the idea of insurance altogether. American Indians are also exempt. Scientologists might want to consider advertising: "Join us and protect your tax refunds!"

EMPLOYER MANDATES

If Scientologists can escape the mandate, businesses can't. Hefty fines will hit employers with more than fifty employees who do not provide their workers federally approved insurance.

An employer of fifty or more workers that did not offer federally approved insurance would have to pay a fine of $2,000 per worker.[5] (Note that the first thirty workers are exempted for purposes of calculating the fine.)

Of course, paying those fines might be cheaper than offering health insurance, so some employers might decide to cancel their existing policies and tell their employees to purchase insurance through the state-based exchanges. According to the Congressional Budget Office (CBO), the number of people with employer-sponsored coverage will drop by 14 million.[6] And where might these newly uninsured Americans find coverage?

EXCHANGES AND SUBSIDIES

Once these mandates, fines, and group-insurance cancellations steer participants into the health-insurance market, they would purchase coverage through state-based Health Benefits Exchanges. Small-business owners would buy insurance through their own system of exchanges.

Accompanying the sticks of mandates and fines, Obamacare also offers carrots in the form of subsidies for buying insurance. Eligibility for these subsidies within the American Health Benefits Exchanges is based on where people stand relative to the Federal Poverty Level (FPL) of $10,830 for individuals and $22,050 for a family of four.[7]

For individuals, subsidies will be available for those making between 133 percent ($14,403) and 400 percent ($43,320) of the FPL. For two parents and two kids, the relevant household income must be between $29,326 and $88,200.

If nearly $90,000 seems like a rather hefty income to merit federal subsidy, this eye-opening sum will grow even more shocking as it rises with inflation.

INSURANCE REGULATIONS

Obamacare will place numerous new regulations on private insurance companies. Among the major changes:

- PR stunt. Effective September 23, 2010, the federal government will forbid insurers from cancelling the health insurance of unhealthy people. (Insurers agreed to voluntarily stop this practice as of May 2010.) Sounds like a reasonable regulation, right? Well, it is—which is why cancelling the insurance of unhealthy people has been illegal in this country for more than a decade. The Obama regulation is merely a PR stunt.

- No lifetime, annual, or dollar caps on benefits. Sounds great—except that it means that cheap insurance plans with very reasonable $2 million limits on coverage will no longer be available; everyone will be shuttled into more expensive plans.

- Also starting on September 23, 2010, parental coverage for sons and daughters will extend into young adulthood. Obamacare requires insurance companies to cover the "children" of policy holders until age twenty-six. Why not twenty-five? Or twenty-seven? Congress does not explain its entitlements numerology, but does promise that further regulation will "define the dependents to which coverage shall be made available." Think about it: according to the Constitution, you can be elected to the House of Representatives at age twenty-five—and you could still be on your parents' health insurance plan! What a country!

- Guaranteed issue. This provision essentially will require insurers to approve 100 percent of health-insurance applications, regardless of the applicant's risky behavior or poor health. This is like forcing Allstate to provide fire insurance to someone who builds a log cabin on a breeze-swept, brush-covered Malibu hillside, even if—at the moment the application arrives—the property happens to be ablaze.

- Community rating. Within a designated geographic area, insurers could adjust the cost of coverage based only on age, family composition, and tobacco use. So two 35-year-old single men occupying the same block in Phoenix would be charged the same price for health insurance, even if one is a trim, teetotaling tennis instructor, and the other is an obese, alcoholic couch potato.

- New government-administered insurance plan. Obamacare requires the Office of Personnel Management—which oversees the federal civil service—to contract with insurers to establish at least two multi-state health plans to be sold through the new state-based exchanges. Many analysts fear that these government-chartered insurance plans could eventually morph into a full-blown public option, where government insurance begins to crowd out the private sector.

FEEDING THE MEDICAID BLOB

Perhaps half of those newly insured under Obamacare will be covered under Medicaid.

Obamacare increases Medicaid eligibility to 133 percent of the Federal Poverty Level, or $29,326 for a family of four, or $14,403 for an individual.

Obamacare also extends Medicaid to childless adults.[8]

In fact, this new law is expected to add 18 million people to the Medicaid rolls bringing the total to 84 million.[9]

Governors and state legislators facing a storm surge of red ink from coast to coast must welcome this news with unbridled glee.

According to Heritage Foundation estimates, debt-soaked California will see its Medicaid enrollment rise 38 percent thanks to Obamacare; in New Jersey, the figure is 55 percent; in Texas, the Medicaid population will swell by 73 percent.

In a sort of welfare reform in reverse, Obamacare will expand the Medicaid rolls by 37 percent.

BOARDS, COMMISSIONS, AND AGENCIES

According to Republican Congressman Tom Price of Georgia (who happens to be a doctor), this federal juggernaut will be administered by no fewer than 159 brand-new boards, commissions, and agencies,[10] most likely with the assistance of dozens of existing federal bureaus.

These new federal organizations include the Patient-Centered Outcomes Research Institute, the Private Purchasing Council, and the Medicaid Emergency Psychiatric Demonstration Project, among scores more.

WHAT'S THE COST?

So, what's all of this supposed to cost? According to the CBO, Obamacare will consume $938 billion between 2010 and 2019. Obamacare's GOP critics argue that because the CBO front-loaded the anticipated tax revenues and backloaded the benefit costs of Obamacare, a more accurate measurement would cover the first ten years that Obamacare is up and running, namely 2014 to 2024, in which case you're looking at bill of about $2.5 trillion.

TAXES, TAXES, AND TAXES

Where on earth will America find that kind of money? Obamacare will be financed by a tornado of new taxes. These $569 billion in new levies include the following items, among others:[11]

- Starting in 2013, individuals earning more than $200,000 and couples making $250,000 or more will see their Medicare Part A tax rise from 1.45 percent to 2.35 percent of income.[12]

- They will also face a brand-new 3.8 percent tax on so-called "unearned income," including investment proceeds from partnerships, royalties, and rents.

- Insurance companies will get hit with $47.5 billion in new taxes between now and 2018. After that, they can expect to pay at least $14.3 billion in taxes a year—costs that will surely make health insurance pricier.

- Pharmaceutical manufacturers will pay $16.7 billion in new taxes through 2019, and then another $2.8 billion a year afterward, in addition to their existing tax liabilities.

- A brand-new 2.3 percent federal tax will apply to the sales of medical devices, such as pacemakers, prosthetic limbs, and insulin pumps for diabetics. This is expected to channel about $2 billion a year away from these innovative, life-saving companies into federal coffers.

- A brand-new 10 percent federal excise tax will hit customers of America's tanning salons. This tax commences on July 1, 2010, pretty much exactly when anyone who wants a tan will get it at the beach, rather than indoors.

- A brand-new 40 percent tax hits so-called Cadillac health plans worth more than $10,200 for individuals and $27,500 for families. This has the unusual effect of giving gold-plated health plans platinum-plated price tags. This contradicts Obama's supposed desire to reduce insurance costs. Also, this tax doesn't hit until 2018. Why so late? Well, that was a concession to union leaders, who will, no doubt, be far out of sight when the shoe drops on their rank and file, who tend to have gold-plated plans.

- Businesses will face vast new income-tax reporting requirements. Starting in 2012, firms must submit a 1099 form for every business at which they spend at least $600. Before Obamacare, companies had to file 1099s only for payments made to independent contractors and certain other service providers. Small businesses in particular will struggle to comply with the dictate, as they'll have to submit hundreds of new forms for their purchases at office-supply stores, restaurants, airlines, and the like.

CUTTING MEDICARE

Obamacare also siphons money away from Medicare—$529 billion-worth over ten years. Never mind that Medicare was already scheduled for bankruptcy around 2017; Obamacare robs Medicare to pay for itself while leaving most of Medicare's existing benefit obligations in place, so, sooner or later, something is going to implode.

Meanwhile, about one quarter of seniors—or about 11 million people—enjoy Medicare Advantage. This flexible, partially private program allows seniors considerable choice in their medical care. Obamacare would chop $202 billion from this popular program beginning in 2011.

Also, Obamacare is expected to lower Medicare's payments to doctors. Medical providers already wait months and even weeks for Medicare's 80-cents-on-the-dollar standard reimbursements. Health professionals are wondering what will happen when even more patients demand more and more care while essentially walking into treatment centers with smaller and smaller payments.

KEEP DREAMING

This huge new entitlement, which features more nooks and crannies than an English muffin, promises to provide insurance to 34 million previously uninsured people.[13] Left unsaid is that despite Obamacare's sweeping scope and stunning cost, an estimated 23 million Americans will *still* be uninsured.[14] So after the creation of 159 new agencies, the promulgation of 2,562 pages of bureaucratic regulations, and the spending of $2.5 trillion in tax dollars, two-thirds of those uninsured still will be. Only in government could that be considered a victory.

CHAPTER 5

UNDERSTANDING THE UNINSURED

Throughout the health care debate of 2009, Democrats repeated *ad nauseum* that there were 46.3 million people in the United States who lacked health insurance,[1] including some 8 million children, and that the only way to deal with this crisis was through government-provided insurance.

That 46.3 million figure comes from the U.S. Census Bureau, which reported in 2009 in its *Current Population Survey* (*CPS*) that the number of people without coverage rose from 45.7 million in 2007 to 46.3 million in 2008. The percentage of the uninsured population remained unchanged at 15.4 percent.[2]

Who makes up these tens of millions counted as uninsured?

It turns out that about 9.7 million people,[3] or 21 percent of the total number of uninsured, earn more than $75,000 a year. They could, in other words, afford to buy health insurance at going rates, but choose not to.

As many as 14 million are eligible for generous government health care programs like Medicare, Medicaid, and the State Children's Health Insurance Program (SCHIP), but choose not to enroll.[4]

Six million people, or 13 percent of the total uninsured, are eligible for employer-sponsored insurance but don't opt in.

Recent legal immigrants, who may not yet have chosen to buy health insurance, number 5 million, or 10.8 percent, of the total.

Finally, 5.2 million illegal immigrants, or 11.2 percent, were counted as without health insurance in the *CPS*.[5]

Assuming some overlap with these numbers, there are, at most, 10 million U.S. citizens who lack affordable health care options, a much less scary figure—especially if we bear in mind that even those who can't afford insurance still have access to health care. Under the Emergency Medical Treatment and Active Labor Act (EMTALA), passed back in 1986, virtually all hospitals must provide emergency care to anyone needing treatment, regardless of citizenship or ability to pay. Contrary to Congresswoman Louise Slaughter's claim that "we have seen hospitals abandon patients to the streets" in recent years, most American hospitals can't and don't turn away patients who need care.[6]

BEHIND THE BIG NUMBER

There are other flaws in the *CPS* figure. Like any large survey, the Census report produces significant margins of error. In

fact, the Census Bureau itself states that "health insurance coverage is likely to be underreported in the *CPS*."

So the survey isn't necessarily precise. But let's suppose that
it is correct. Many people assume that if 46.3 million people are
uninsured, they're chronically uninsured. But that's not the
case. The Census Bureau reports that "the *CPS*... estimate of
the number of people without health insurance more closely
approximates the number of people who were uninsured at a
specific point in time" rather than people who were uninsured
for the entire year."[7]

That suggests that many of the people who were counted as
"uninsured" may have only been experiencing a short-term
interruption in their health coverage. This would have been
particularly true when the latest survey was conducted, during
the recession of 2008, when companies cut back on benefits,
and many Americans lost their jobs. Even in good times, it's
common for people to be temporarily uninsured as they leave
and switch jobs.

In fact, reliance on employer-based insurance has been
one of the fundamental problems in our health care system.
Employers get a tax break for covering employees, and these
employees get their health insurance with pre-tax dollars. Of
course, their wages are lower because employers factor the
cost of insurance into their payroll plans. Individuals who
buy their own insurance, on the other hand, get no tax break
at all. In addition to being unfair, this makes the whole system heavily dependent on employment—which ensures that
problems with access to health care will be exacerbated in
any recession.

Unfortunately, the health care bill that became law in 2010 doesn't fix this problem. Employers are still able to buy health insurance with pre-tax dollars, with individuals only able to buy with post-tax dollars. Many Americans remain heavily dependent on employer-sponsored insurance. (We'll delve into this problem in greater detail later.)

In addition to job-hunters and job-changers, young people first entering the job market are also likely to be uninsured. That's unfortunate, but the big number obscures the fact that they are not chronically uninsured. They tend to acquire insurance when they find better jobs or make more money.

The Census reported that there are 8.2 million 18- to 24-year-olds without insurance, or 17.7 percent of the total uninsured, and that there are 10.8 million 25- to 34-year-olds without insurance, or 23.3 percent.[8] By contrast, those under eighteen number 7.4 million, or 16 percent of the uninsured, and those over sixty-five number only 646,000, or 1.4 percent.[9]

In short, to suggest that 46.3 million Americans are chronically uninsured is a big stretch. As we've seen from the breakdown of the numbers and the Census's own reports, fewer than 10 million Americans have no access to insurance, and for many of those it may be a temporary circumstance.

There are other ways in which the Census figure is widely misunderstood. Let's break down the numbers further.

THE VOLUNTARILY UNINSURED

We've seen that 9.7 million Americans who make more than $75,000 a year choose not to buy health insurance. Another

8 million make between $50,000 and $74,999 a year.[10] That means that 38.2 percent of the uninsured make more than $50,000 a year, or an above-average income. These numbers belie the argument that the uninsured are members of down-and-out, low-income families.

You can bet that most of those who choose to forego health insurance are willing to pony up for other life necessities. They buy groceries, take vacations, and purchase car insurance. So why are they skipping out on health insurance?

Quite a few are what the health care industry calls the "invincibles." They're young and childless, between the ages of nineteen and twenty-nine, and convinced that they're unlikely to get sick—or at least convinced enough that they'd rather take the risk of foregoing insurance, and instead pocket the money they'd otherwise have spent on monthly premiums. If they do get sick or have to go to the hospital, they pay out of pocket.[11]

Given the high cost of health insurance, taking this risk can be an entirely rational choice. Still, many uninsured people would no doubt buy insurance if it were cheaper—and the way to make insurance cheaper is to encourage greater market competition. Unfortunately, Obamacare takes the opposite approach—stifling competition through increased government regulation.

ILLEGAL IMMIGRANTS

In the Census total of 46.3 million uninsured, about 5.2 million, or 11.2 percent of the total, are illegal immigrants.[12] If we include legal residents, the number of uninsured non-citizens jumps to 9.5 million people.[13]

These people can still get health care by visiting hospital emergency rooms—and they often do. Or they can pay out of pocket at a regular doctor's office or clinic. But their problem is less a health insurance problem than an immigration reform problem—and that is a separate issue altogether.

THE LOW-INCOME UNINSURED

So what about the 10 million (or perhaps fewer) Americans who truly can't afford health care? Well, as many as 14 million Americans are eligible for existing government-run programs like Medicare, which covers the elderly, Medicaid, which covers low-income citizens, and SCHIP, which is designed to cover children from low- and middle-income families who fall through the cracks.

The problem is that many eligible low-income Americans are not enrolling in these programs.

As Dr. David Gratzer has written, "You may think that a poor single mom with three children living in South Central Los Angeles is among the uninsured, but in fact, she is eligible for Medicaid, as are her children... these individuals could be covered; they just choose not to do the paperwork."[14] Medicaid and children's health programs allow patients literally to sign up in the emergency room.[15]

A study by the Urban Institute found that about 27 percent of non-elderly Americans who were eligible for Medicaid hadn't enrolled.[16] And a 2008 study by the Georgetown University Health Policy Institute found that a full 70 percent of uninsured children were eligible for either SCHIP or Medicaid or both.[17]

When calling for national health care reform, Obama often mentioned the "nearly eight million children" lacking health insurance. He didn't mention that 5 million could have been enrolled in health insurance plans, but weren't.

The failure to enroll in available programs indicates some sort of problem. It may be that participation should be made easier, though it is already quite easy. Or it may be that many people don't enroll because they know it's extremely difficult to find a primary care doctor who accepts Medicaid patients. This is because Medicaid reimbursement rates for doctors are much lower than those paid by private insurers.

WHO'S LEFT?

Sadly, there really are people who fall through the cracks. They are the working poor who have been chronically uninsured. They've held down jobs, generally earning less than $50,000 a year, but too much to qualify for government help. They haven't been able to afford to buy health insurance at going rates. They've had some access to health care in the form of emergency room visits and community hospitals, but they haven't been covered for the preventative care that might have kept them out of the hospital in the first place. They really do need help. Any attempt to solve the problem of the uninsured should focus on these people.

What they need is basic, affordable insurance to cover catastrophes. That is, they need insurance plans with a low monthly premium and a high deductible. Such plans wouldn't pay for everything from eyewear to acupuncture, as some state laws require, but they would be affordable and provide benefits in health emergencies so that a medical disaster doesn't also become a financial one.

Instead, Obamacare lays on more government bureaucracy, regulation, and taxes that will only raise rates—indeed, heavy regulation is why health insurance is so expensive in the first place.

OBAMA'S CAMPAIGN

Obama's campaign website said, "Forty-six million Americans—including nearly eight million children—lack health insurance with no signs of this trend slowing down."[18] As president, in August 2009, as the health care debate was heating up, he said, "I don't have to explain to you that nearly 46 million Americans don't have health insurance coverage today. In the wealthiest nation on Earth, 46 million of our fellow citizens have no coverage. They are just vulnerable. If something happens, they go bankrupt, or they don't get the care they need."[19]

Obama either profoundly misunderstood or misrepresented the health care problem in the United States. He also often claimed that the number of uninsured Americans was rising, which was true in raw terms, but, more important, false in terms of their percentage of the total population, and doubly misleading because the circumstances of low-income uninsured Americans has gotten better, not worse, over the last decade. The number of households with annual incomes of less than $25,000 lacking health insurance went steadily down from 1998 to 2007[20] and remained unchanged between 2007 and 2008.[21]

So do we have a health care crisis of uninsured Americans? Well, yes, because even if fewer than 10 million American citizens lack affordable health insurance, that's 10 million too many. But the "crisis" is far less dramatic than the one put forward by Obama and his allies; and, ironically, it's a problem that Obamacare does little to fix.

CHAPTER 6

HEALTH CARE SPENDING ISN'T A DISEASE

I t's no surprise that many Americans think health care spending is out of control. At 17.3 percent of the GDP, the United States spends more on health care than any other rich country. Switzerland comes in second at 11.5 percent. France, Belgium, and Canada each spend 10 percent. And Japan and Great Britain spend 7.5 percent.[1] Though to put this in some perspective, the average American consumer spent $2,853 on health care in 2009, which is the same amount he spent on eating out.[2]

Still, it's true that health care spending is accelerating.

In 1960, just $148 was spent on health care per person per year, or 5.2 percent of GDP. Only $111 of that was spent by individuals out-of-pocket; the rest was paid for with public funds.[3] By 2008, total health spending in the United States was $7,681 per person per year, with $4,046 of that spent, on average, by individuals.[4]

That's a pretty big increase in spending over five decades.

It's easy to see why Americans look at these numbers and wonder what happened as they express increasing unhappiness over their doctors' bills. And it's just as easy to see why politicians have struggled, in administration after administration, to devise a solution, and why Obama was able to convince enough Democrats that his overhaul of the health care system was necessary. But it's a myth that we spend too much on health care; the fact is, Americans spend more on health care than do citizens of other countries because we get better health care—and we demand it, too.

THE COST OF LIFE

You've heard countless politicians bemoan the soaring costs of health care—but have you ever heard one of them mention the dramatic gains we've made in health care? We all know that medical science has made huge advances—and those advances need to be figured into the costs. The difference between cost and value can be the difference between life and death.

Let's suppose a young woman is diagnosed with breast cancer. The cancer is caught relatively early, and she's treated with a combination of chemotherapy and radiation therapy—both of which have become radically more sophisticated in recent decades.

Deaths from breast cancer have dropped steadily since 1990 because of earlier detection and better treatments.[5] According to the American Cancer Society's most recent numbers, patients with stage 4 breast cancer, widely seen as "incurable," now have a 20 percent 5-year survival rate, while those with stage 1 breast cancer have a 100 percent 5-year survival rate. (While the data tally patients who live at least five years after being diagnosed, many live much longer.)[6]

Our young woman finds herself completely cured. She owes her life to the miracle of modern medicine. It cost her and her insurer a lot of money.

But who's to say it wasn't worth it?

The value she got from her treatments is immeasurable. After all, the cost of a treatment, however expensive, is not truly low if you end up paying with your life—or with a reduction in your quality of life.

Do you know anyone who's undergone lower-back surgery within the past few years? Chances are that person would have been permanently crippled fifty years ago.

When we talk about how to change our health care system—or when we criticize it—we also need to understand what's working well. We should recognize the tremendous strides that have been made in medicine over the last seventy years.

These advances haven't been cheap, but most of us probably know someone who is alive or healthier today because of them.

THE GREAT LEAP FORWARD IN VALUE

Consider advances made since the first half of the twentieth century.

Penicillin, administered for the first time in 1941 to treat a patient ravaged by an infection from a scratch, transformed the medical landscape dramatically.[7]

After that, the breakthroughs came in rapid succession:

Cortisone in 1949—it reduces pain, is used in treating arthritis and asthma (among other ailments), and has helped enable organ transplants.

In 1950, doctors found a cure for tuberculosis.

In 1955, medical researcher Jonas Salk's polio vaccine was announced to the world and licensed. It's hard to over-emphasize just how terrifying polio was to Americans until then. Annual epidemics killed thousands and paralyzed tens of thousands.

Then came open-heart surgery, kidney transplantation, and cures for various kinds of cancer. Antibiotics and lithium also came along in the latter half of the twentieth century.[8]

Doctors say that half of all medical treatments in use today were invented in the last twenty-five years.[9]

Former Vice President Dick Cheney is a walking testament to how far we've come on heart disease. Love him or hate him, modern medicine enabled him to continue in public life.

From 2001 to 2009, Cheney completed two terms as vice president—despite having suffered four heart attacks, the first when he was just thirty-seven. By the time he entered office, he'd had quadruple bypass surgery and an angioplasty—and in 2001 he received a pacemaker. He had a fifth heart attack in 2010,[10] but has nevertheless continued a robust career of speaking and writing.

The death rate from heart attack and heart failure fell by more than 50 percent between 1950 and 2000, from 307 per 100,000 to 126.[11] And over the last two decades, survival periods after heart failure have steadily increased.[12] Those changes have meant that someone who would likely have died young sixty years ago could go on being a productive—in Cheney's case, a highly productive—member of society.

KEEPING COSTS IN PERSPECTIVE

Salk began searching for a polio vaccine in 1948. He assembled a highly skilled team of researchers and devoted himself to the cause for the next seven years. The first field trial to test his discovery was among the most elaborate that had ever been conducted. It involved 20,000 doctors and public health officials, as well as 64,000 school staffers and 220,000 volunteers.[13]

There's no estimate of how much it cost to successfully develop the vaccine, though clearly a great deal of time and money was required. The result was a dramatic decline in polio, even before the next vaccine came along in 1961.

Today the disease has been nearly eradicated. Whatever the cost, that's a pretty good return on investment.

Today it's estimated that the average cost of developing a single new drug, from lab research through clinical trials, is around $1.3 billion.

Or consider that pacemaker Cheney has in his chest, a special kind called an implantable cardioverter defibrillator, or ICD.[14]

Having one installed usually cost tens of thousands of dollars, and sometimes more than $100,000.[15]

As physician Dr. David Gratzer observes, "The little box in the chest of the vice president costs more than fifty times what the average American spent on health care (adjusted for inflation) for an entire year in 1950."[16]

In short, it costs money to keep people alive.

In 1954, it cost nothing to prevent polio, because there was no way to do so. You just became paralyzed or died. Likewise, the standard treatment for heart attack in the early twentieth century was bed rest. It came cheap, but the prognosis wasn't good.

Medical innovation was the main driver of health care costs over the second half of the twentieth century. (Other causes were an aging population, increasing disposable income, and expanding insurance coverage.)[17]

IT'S WORTH IT

The size of your health care bill means nothing unless you also look at what kind of bang you're getting for the buck. We pay more for health care today because we have treatments that work.

American life expectancy increased by thirty years over the course of the twentieth century. If you were a male born in 1900, there was an 18 percent chance you'd be dead by your first birthday. By 2005, the cumulative mortality rate didn't reach 18 percent until age sixty-two.[18]

Our improvement in health can also be measured in terms of mortality. In 2009, the U.S. death rate was 7.9 per 1,000 people.[19] That's a 16.8 percent drop from 1950, when the figure was 9.5 per 1,000 people.[20]

Meanwhile, the average American life expectancy has increased by more than ten years since 1950.[21]

Those who constantly cite rising health care costs invariably fail to mention our massive improvements in overall health.

THE RETURN ON INVESTMENT

How do you put a number on a dramatic fall in the mortality rate—or an increased life expectancy? How do you calculate the worth of medical advances that drive these numbers?

It may seem impossible to quantify the true value of improved health care. But in fact, as costs have risen, economists have tried to do just that.

They've found several different ways to calculate the benefits, both for individuals and society at large. Craig Garthwaite, a professor in the Kellogg School of Management at Northwestern University, set out to determine the impact of Vioxx, a drug approved by the FDA in 1999 to treat arthritis and acute pain.

Vioxx was withdrawn from the market in 2004 due to potential negative side effects. The quick arrival and disappearance of Vioxx makes it useful as a case study.

Garthwaite set out to discover just how many people Vioxx kept in the work force since health, physical and mental, is a key factor in determining whether people can stay in the labor force.

And staying in the labor force has many positive results—boosting one's livelihood being the most obvious.

In the bigger picture, the continued ability to work means fewer people receiving disability payments, lowering the amount paid out in taxpayer dollars. And a greater labor supply keeps businesses healthy too.

Garthwaite found that men between the ages of fifty-five and sixty-one with joint conditions were 12 percent more likely to be able to work if they took Vioxx; and men who worked in physically demanding jobs had even better results.[22]

As Garthwaite points out, "Vioxx is only one example of a medical innovation that may have demonstrable economic impacts. Other innovations such as improved treatments for heart attack victims, joint replacements, and new prescription medications addressing a wide variety of chronic conditions, may also improve the economic livelihood of individuals."[23]

Economists have also sought to calculate the true cost of various treatments. In a 2008 study, Mark Duggan of the University of Maryland and William Evans of the University of Notre Dame sought to figure out the true cost of HIV anti-retroviral treatments (ARVs).[24]

Using readily available data from Medicaid, they estimated that ARVs had reduced mortality from HIV by 70 percent, and lowered the amount patients had to spend to deal with other ailments. "Combining these two effects," they write, "we estimate the cost per life year saved at $22,000."[25]

Twenty-two thousand dollars to live another year. Would you pay that much? My guess is that many of those whose lives were saved wouldn't consider it excessive.

Similar studies have found similar results. For example, trials in Europe found that administering tissue plasminogen activator (t-PA) after a heart attack provided an extra year of life at a cost of $33,000.[26]

And it's not just a year of life that is saved. Younger patients who survive thanks to these treatments, according to Nobel Prize-winning economist Gary S. Becker, "tend to have better survivorship rates at older ages too,"[27] because they tend to develop beneficial habits: not discounting the future, getting more education, and thus achieving higher earnings.

SHOULD MEDICINE BE FREE?

Imagine that you were at death's door, and I offered you a $20,000 pill that gave you another twenty years of life. That means that it would cost you $1,000 a year to keep living. Most Americans would call that a pretty good deal.

Unfortunately, most Americans aren't used to thinking about medicine that way. That's because we don't usually pay for our health care directly. Instead, a third party pays—often the insurance company providing us subsidized health insurance through an employer, or the government.

As a result, we tend to think that health care isn't subject to the same laws of economics as the other things we purchase, like tickets to the movies or automobiles. We're perfectly happy to pay $20,000, or more, for a new car—and it's not likely to last twenty years.

WHAT WE REALLY SPEND

To really put things in perspective, let's look at how health care bills compare to our other expenditures. Democrats bemoaned the rising cost of health care, which was why government had to get more involved. But, in fact, the percentage of household spending that goes to health care has changed very little.

Americans spent only 5.9 percent of their total household expenditures on health care in 2008, according to data from the Bureau of Labor Statistics.[28] That's significantly less than what they spent on food (12.8 percent), transportation including both cars and gasoline (17 percent), or housing (33.9 percent).[29]

In fact, the closest comparable figure in total household expenditures is the amount spent on entertainment, 5.6 percent. Spending on par with entertainment suggests that Americans can afford health care after all.

What about the myth of rising health care costs?

In 1989, Americans spent 5.1 percent of household expenditures on health care.[30] Ten years later, in 1999, they spent 5.3 percent.[31] By 2003, they were spending 5.9 percent.[32] And that number has remained unchanged.

In other words, as a percentage of total expenditures, health care spending has risen less than 1 percent since 1989. (At the time of publication, 2008 was the last year for which the Bureau of Labor Statistics had data.)

While health care costs have increased in financial terms, in two decades they've barely increased as a percentage of what we spend.

OBAMA AND THE MYTH

Unfortunately, it seems that just as Barack Obama bought into the myth that more than 15 percent of Americans couldn't get health care, he also bought into the myth that health care is too expensive.

In early 2008, he suggested that the biggest problem in health care was affordability. "The problem is not that folks are trying to avoid getting health care; the problem is they can't afford it. My plan emphasizes lowering costs."[33]

A year later, as president, he continued in the same vein. In his 2009 State of the Union address, Obama declared, "We must also address the crushing cost of health care. This is a cost that now causes a bankruptcy in America every 30 seconds."

Actually, thanks to FactCheck.org, which crunched the numbers, we know that's not true.[34] There were about 934,000 personal bankruptcies in 2008, and there are about 32 million seconds in a year. Even if half of those were due to medical expenses, which is unlikely, that would amount to one health-related bankruptcy a minute, or half the number Obama suggested.[35] Given that many bankruptcies in 2008 were due to home foreclosures and a worsening economy, the number was probably much lower.

Moreover, if high health care costs were a driving force behind bankruptcy, then countries with socialized medicine (or "single-payer" systems) would have fewer bankruptcies. But that's not the case.

According to a study by Canada's Fraser Institute, the personal bankruptcy rate was higher in Canada than it was in the United States in 2006 and 2007. In fact, the study showed that "non-medical expenditures comprise the majority of debt among bankrupt consumers in both Canada and the US."[36]

Okay, so someone on Obama's team didn't check the facts. That may seem like a small mistake—but it also suggests a cavalier willingness to accept—or promote—the notion that health care costs are "too high" simply because it advances your agenda, regardless of whether it is true.

The fact is we're not spending too much on health care, any more than we spend too much on food, shelter, or transportation. In recent decades, health care expenses have increased only incrementally as a percentage of total personal spending, while at the same time our health care technology has improved dramatically.

Obamacare, unfortunately, threatens to take that incredible progress and stifle it with the heavy hand of government bureaucracy, regulation, and taxation. That's a bad trade.

THE WRONG DIAGNOSIS,
THE WRONG TREATMENTS

In the chapters that follow, we'll look at a dozen of the most significant of the hundreds of regulatory components that pepper Obamacare. Each of these regulations threatens to transform America's health care system in ways that are truly harmful; and we'll show exactly why and debunk the flawed logic behind them.

CHAPTER 7

CONGRATULATIONS! YOU'RE NOW ON MEDICAID!

As we've seen, part of Obamacare is a massive expansion of Medicaid,[1] a program that was created by the federal government in 1965 to provide a health care safety net for the truly poor.

Since Medicaid is administered at the state level, each state's program is slightly different. However, they are all overseen by a federal agency, the Centers for Medicare and Medicaid Services (CMS). They are also funded only in part by the federal government. The rest is paid out of state coffers.

Medicaid is a means-tested program. So it doesn't simply cover all people with low incomes. Other eligibility standards (such as age, assets, dependents, and disabilities) come into play.

Today, if you're a healthy 30-year-old with no dependent children, you probably wouldn't qualify for Medicaid assistance, regardless of your income.

As of 2014, that will change. Under Obamacare, all state Medicaid programs will be required to cover most people who earn up to 133 percent of the federal poverty level.[2]

In today's dollars, that means an individual who earns $14,404 or less would qualify for Medicaid, and a family earning $29,326 or less would qualify.[3]

As of 2008, Medicaid covered 43 million people, or 14 percent of the population.[4] Under the new law, it will soon cover more than 60 million. CMS estimates that this will cost about $410 billion.[5]

ALREADY COVERING THE TRULY POOR

According to the latest count from the U.S. Census, nearly 40 million people in the United States live below the federal poverty level. The figure rose in both raw numbers and percentage terms between 2007 and 2008, from 12.5 percent of the total population to 13.2 percent. The poverty rate for blacks, Latinos, and children under eighteen is significantly higher.[6]

It is certainly true that people living in poverty need access to health care, but it is absolutely false that the way to do that is by massively expanding government health care programs. The fact is, most truly poor Americans already had access to government health care long before Obamacare was passed in March 2010. The "poor" people who don't qualify are frequently healthy adults under sixty-five with no dependents who simply choose not to work—or have substantial assets.

In 2008, federal outlays on Medicaid were about $204 billion—and the federal government pays only 57 percent of Medicaid expenses, with states picking up the rest. That year, Medicaid provided coverage to roughly 43 million people, or substantially more than the number of Americans living in poverty.[7]

Meanwhile, children from low-income families that don't qualify for Medicaid are eligible for coverage under the State Children's Health Insurance Plan, or SCHIP. Under the 2008 federal budget, SCHIP was reauthorized for five years, over which time new federal outlays were expected to total $5 billion.[8]

Finally, the poor also receive health care under the Emergency Medical Treatment and Active Labor Act, in effect since 1986. Under that law, hospitals must treat anyone who walks into an emergency room for an injury or disease, regardless of ability to pay. The costs of such care are absorbed into hospitals' operating costs.

The trouble is that such government programs, and particularly Medicaid, have failed again and again to provide the level of care available in the private sector. Before we expand Medicaid, we should take a hard look at how its patients are faring.

SUBSTANDARD CARE

Medicaid has been around nearly half a century, giving us plenty of information on how, as a government-run program, it stacks up against private-sector health care. Let's start at the most basic level and compare outcomes.

If you have a heart attack and you're covered by Medicaid, your chances of recovery are significantly lower than if you're covered by either private insurance or by Medicare. That was the finding of a 2006 study published in the *Annals of Internal Medicine*.

To be sure, poor patients covered under Medicaid tend to be sicker, and may have received less preventative care over the course of their lives—but those factors suggest that Medicaid wasn't taking good care of them in the first place.

The study's authors found that heart attack outcomes were worse for Medicaid patients even after adjusting for other factors, like education, illnesses, and the type of facility where the patient received treatment. The most important predictor of outcome, in other words, was whether the patient had Medicaid.[9]

Another study, published in 2009 in the journal *Psychiatric Services*, found that state Medicaid practices intended to save money were associated with worse outcomes among mentally ill patients.

The study looked at more than 1,600 patients in ten states. Medicaid policies—like mandating the use of generics, limiting doses, and requiring prior authorization for prescriptions—meant that mentally ill patients had trouble getting access to medicine, which made them 3.6 times more likely to experience a "significant adverse event." Those included emergency room visits, hospitalizations, homelessness, suicidal behavior, and incarceration.

States' attempts to save money on Medicaid, in other words, came with a high cost to society and enormous personal pain.[10]

DODGED BY DOCTORS

Medicaid patients often find that few doctors are willing to see them because Medicaid payments to doctors are so low.

Many doctors are small entrepreneurs, operating solo or in group practices. They live on what their businesses bring in. More and more are simply opting out of accepting Medicaid because the patients don't cover costs.

The federal government only partly funds Medicaid. Cash-strapped states must also pay, and many are finding it increasingly difficult to do so. That's because as the program grows, it becomes more expensive. Even before Obamacare, Medicaid enrollment was already growing rapidly. Between June 2008 and June 2009, Medicaid saw a record 7.5 percent increase in patients covered—shooting up to 47 million.[11]

To meet their growing budget shortfalls, state capitals have begun looking for ways to limit Medicaid spending. Many of them are cutting payments to doctors—sometimes to shockingly low rates.

In Michigan, Medicaid payments to primary care physicians can now be less than $25 per visit. A Michigan obstetrician told the *New York Times* that she receives $29 from Medicaid for a visit that would earn her $70 from Blue Cross/Blue Shield of Michigan, a private insurer.[12]

Doctors are typically paid up to $260 for an hour-long consultation with a patient who has private insurance.

But in New York state, physicians earn just $20 for a consultation with an established Medicaid patient.[13] That's less than a class at a yoga studio—and doctors can face significantly more in overhead, from nurses' salaries to medical equipment to liability insurance.

With fees like that, many doctors lose money every time a Medicaid patient walks into the room. As a result, fewer and fewer are accepting Medicaid payments.

A 2009 survey found that just 38.6 percent of physicians in Dallas participated in the program.[14] Meanwhile, statewide, the proportion of Texas doctors accepting all new Medicaid patients tumbled from 67 percent to 42 percent in the decade prior to 2010.[15]

In Idaho, only 39 percent of primary care doctors in urban areas will see Medicaid patients now.[16]

In a nationwide survey of physicians conducted in 2008, the Center for Studying Health System Change found that 28 percent of doctors were accepting no new Medicaid patients.[17]

Underpayments don't even begin to account for the countless hours doctors spend filling out government forms to comply with the thousands of pages of Medicaid regulations. By consuming the time of doctors' staffs, Medicaid paperwork drives up costs to doctors even further.

In short, doctors are opting out because if they didn't, Medicaid would put them out of business. As a result, Medicaid patients often have an extremely difficult time finding a doctor.

In May 2010, the Centers for Disease Control and Prevention (CDC) released a report which found that among Medicaid patients under sixty-five, more than 30 percent had visited an emergency room at least once in 2007. By contrast, fewer than 20 percent of people with private insurance made a trip to the emergency room that year.[18] "High Medicaid utilization is no surprise, many patients have difficulty finding primary care providers who take Medicaid, so the ER is the only alternative," said Frank McGeorge, an ER physician quoted in *USA Today* on the CDC study.[19]

As Medicaid patients increasingly turn to emergency rooms for routine care, it puts hospitals in a serious financial bind. Unlike doctors, hospitals are less able to opt out of Medicaid altogether. Not only does Medicaid pay less than private insurers—it often pays less than the cost of care.

In a 2009 study, the American Hospital Association found that 56 percent of hospitals received Medicaid payments that didn't cover the expense involved in delivering care.

These underpayments are on the rise: Total underpayments to hospitals rose from $3.8 billion in 2000 to $32 billion in 2008.[20]

SHIFTING THE BURDEN

When doctors and hospitals continue to take Medicaid, they have to do something to make up lost revenue and stay in business. So they shift the costs onto patients who are paying with Medicare, private insurance, or their own cash.

Doctors and hospitals have to cover their costs somehow. So when the government pays artificially low prices, costs go up for everyone else.

A study in the journal *Health Affairs* found that, nationally, Medicaid pays 92 cents for each dollar its beneficiaries consume.[21] Hospitals alone, according to the American Hospital Association, receive 89 cents for every dollar spent caring for Medicaid patients.[22]

Studies have estimated just how much of the burden is being shifted from the public to the private sector, and the amounts are enormous.

A New America Foundation study found that people with private insurance pay 22 percent more than necessary to make up for the public sector's shortfall.[23]

Stanford business professor Daniel P. Kessler, meanwhile, looked at hospitals in California to try to understand the level of cost-shifting. "Cost shifting from Medicare and Medi-Cal [the Medicaid program in California] is substantial," Kessler found. If the government paid its way, he concluded, private insurance holders could have paid 10.8 percent less with no effect on the revenues of health care providers.

The independent consulting group Milliman also studied the cost-shift burden in research published in 2008. Milliman examined payments made by Medicare, Medicaid, and private insurers to physicians and hospitals across the United States.

Milliman found that Medicaid shifted $16.2 billion in hospital costs (in 2006) and $23.7 billion in physician costs (in 2007) directly onto private payers.

That means that Medicaid paid $39.9 billion less than it would have if all payers paid equivalent rates.[24] If there were no cost shift, private payments to hospitals and physicians would have been 15 percent lower.

Such high costs force private insurers to raise premiums. By how much? Milliman crunched the numbers and found that the cost shift adds $1,512 annually, or 10.6 percent, to the premium of a family of four.[25]

UNSUSTAINABLE FOR STATES

Despite underpaying hospitals and doctors, Medicaid's costs are spiraling out of control. In fact, it's on the verge of bankrupting state governments around the country.

Despite an infusion of extra federal money under the American Recovery and Reinvestment Act (ARRA) of 2009—which distributes $87 billion to states in Medicaid funds over nine quarters—state budgets are buckling.[26]

States face increasing demand for Medicaid, even as tax revenues are falling, and most were already facing the likelihood of Medicaid cutbacks by mid 2010. That would probably mean further cuts to rates paid to doctors and hospitals, as well as cuts to benefits and eligibility.[27]

Even with cuts already implemented in early 2010, many states still have big budget deficits they have to close. In fact, some of those with the worst budget shortfalls, like California, Pennsylvania, and Michigan, also have some of the biggest Medicaid outlays.

California is in dire economic straits, with a looming budget gap of more than $20 billion through 2011.[28] It spent $38.3 billion on Medicaid in 2008, including state and federal funds, the highest dollar amount in the nation. (The state portion alone was $12.7 billion.)

Meanwhile, Pennsylvania spent $17.8 billion in 2008, the third-highest amount in the nation, and Michigan spent $9.8 billion, the ninth-highest amount.[29]

In most states, Medicaid is among the top three budget items. On average, states spend about 22 percent of their budgets on Medicaid.[30]

MEDICAID FRAUD

Despite recent efforts to crack down, Medicaid is riddled with fraud.

At the highest level, states have an incentive to bilk the federal government. Since they receive open-ended matching funds from Washington, some use state money that is ostensibly going to Medicaid for other purposes.

One report from the Government Accountability Office found that, in Oregon, supposed Medicaid funds were being used to finance educational programs and non-Medicaid health programs.

In February 2002, the Oregon state legislature misallocated about $131 million in Medicaid money to education.

The same report found that from 2001 to 2003, Pennsylvania somehow ended up with $2.4 billion in "excessive" federal Medicaid matching funds. More than half of Pennsylvania's federal Medicaid funds were put to non-Medicaid uses.[31]

Lower down the fraud food chain, care providers submit claims to Medicaid for services that were never rendered.

In May 2010, police arrested the owner of a New Jersey mental health and substance abuse counseling center, alleging that he had received hundreds of thousands of dollars from Medicaid for fraudulent claims—and that he had offered kickbacks to patients in the form of grocery store gift certificates.[32]

And in April 2010, police arrested the New Jersey owner of a home health care agency on charges that he had fraudulently billed Medicaid for nearly $5 million.[33]

Over in Pennsylvania, auditors found that the state agency that administers Medicaid incorrectly approved benefits to 1,600 of 11,700 randomly selected Medicaid recipients between January 2005 and March 2008—a 13.6 percent error rate.[34]

The cost of erroneous claims by just that one small sample of recipients amounted to $3.3 million.

In Maryland, officials estimate that between 5 and 10 percent of the state's $6 billion in Medicaid is fraudulent.[35]

In 2009, officials opened more than 1,000 new health care fraud investigations.[36] That's a welcome development, but it's not clear that law enforcement can keep up.

Because different states have different auditing and enforcement practices, it's hard to know how much is lost every year to misuse of Medicaid funds, though nationwide a common estimate is at least 10 percent of outlays.[37] In total, health care fraud—including claims made to private insurers and other public agencies—bamboozles taxpayers and the government out of $65 billion a year.[38]

To make matters worse, those figures don't include the increasingly common phenomenon of "Medicaid for Millionaires."

Nearly 80 percent of residents in nursing facilities for the elderly now rely on Medicaid or Medicare subsidies. If that seems like a lot, it is.

More and more seniors are using clever estate planning to protect their assets, and a whole industry of lawyers has sprung up to help them. They advise the elderly to, for instance, transfer away assets at least five years before they think they might enter a nursing home, because that's as far back as the law will look, and they advise clients on what assets will be left out of Medicaid's means test calculations.[39] The result is that more and more middle class and even wealthy Americans are relying on taxpayers to fund their end-of-life care. It's all perfectly legal, but it's an abuse of the system—leaving far fewer resources for the poor.

WHAT NOT TO DO

Clearly, Medicaid is not a good model for health care reform. It delivers poor service, it's riddled with fraud, and it's pushing state budgets deep into the red. If anything, Medicaid should be completely overhauled—or scaled down. Instead, Obamacare has set in motion a massive expansion.

Americans will soon find out that Medicaid is not the cure for our nation's health care woes. It's part of the disease—and it's spreading.

CHAPTER 8

SHACKLED TO THE MANDATE GURNEY

The idea of forcing everyone to buy health insurance has been around for years; the logic behind the idea is that such a law would guarantee universal coverage. Suddenly, all Americans would have access to great medical care. But passing such a law doesn't just make something so, especially when that law requires people to spend their hard-earned cash.

THE GREAT FLIP-FLOP

Obama was not originally in the "individual mandate" camp. As a presidential candidate, he assured Americans he *wouldn't* include an individual mandate in his health care plan.

In a January 2008 primary debate, he said, "You can mandate [health insurance], but there's still going to be people who can't afford it. And if they cannot afford it, then the question is, what are you going to do about it? Are you going to fine them?"[1]

As it turns out, the answer is yes.

As president, Obama changed his position, and Obamacare now includes an individual mandate. It's a policy rife with problems.

First of all, it's meant to be enforced by a fine. Starting in 2014, everyone has to purchase health insurance or face an annual fine. By 2016, the fine will be at least $695 or 2.5 percent of income to a maximum penalty of $2,085.[2] For all that the individual mandate will cost, it's unlikely to have the desired effect.

The highest penalty works out to $173 a month, and for most people, it will be much lower. Insurance is likely to cost a lot more, so we can expect plenty of people to simply skip insurance and pay the fine.

The IRS, charged with enforcement, will be able to reduce or cancel the tax refunds of anyone who doesn't comply. The new powers granted to the IRS will require new expenditures of taxpayer funds, to the tune of $5 to $10 billion over the next ten years,[3] and the hiring of up to 16,500 new employees.[4]

So much for universal coverage and cutting costs.

THE MANDATE MESS

To understand why an individual mandate won't get us to universal coverage, let's explore why people don't buy health insurance in the first place.

Democratic reformers believe that people who don't buy insurance are either irrational, irresponsible, or too poor. If that were true, a mandate might actually make some sense. But none of those reasons holds water.

For one thing, most of the 46.3 million uninsured people in this country are not the poor. Most low-income Americans and seniors are eligible for health insurance through Medicaid, Medicare, and SCHIP.

The fact is many Americans without health insurance are simply choosing not to buy it. And far from being unwise or irresponsible, they often have perfectly rational reasons. They've done the math, and they don't want to pay for expensive insurance policies that don't fit their needs.

People who don't buy health insurance fall into two major groups.

On the one hand, there are those who earn too much money to qualify for Medicaid, but don't get insurance through an employer and can't afford what's available.

The second, larger group is made up of those who could afford insurance but forego it. A full 38 percent of the uninsured make more than $50,000 a year, an above-average income.[5]

The bottom line is people don't want to pay for what they don't use.

Some of those who opt out are the so-called "invincibles," young people who are willing to bet that they won't get sick.

Consider a 25-year-old man who has just entered the job market, but whose employer doesn't provide him with health coverage. Insurance for a single person can easily cost $400 a month, or $4,800 a year. Our young man could very well decide that's too much to pay for the little medical attention he needs. If he wanted to go for a physical, he could pay the doctor directly and it would still cost a small fraction of an annual insurance bill.

It's easy to see why he would decide that buying health insurance is a waste of money. He's not stupid. He can see that he should have a so-called "catastrophic" policy, or one with a low premium and a high deductible, to save him and his family from financial ruin in case of the worst.

But guess what? Catastrophic policies are very difficult to find. State-level laws and regulations prevent insurers from selling policies that cater to the young and healthy.

There are nearly 2,000 state mandates dictating what health insurance policies must cover, and the list is expansive. (We'll delve deeper into these mandates in the following chapter.)

These mandates drive up the cost of insurance for everyone. Faced with the choice between high-priced insurance and none at all, our young man may choose to go the latter route and put his money into something he deems more important—perhaps textbooks, entertainment, or rent. The point is it's his money.

Under Obamacare, though, the law will attempt to coerce young people to pay their "fair share" of unnecessarily expensive plans.

A COVERT TAX

The insurance mandate is really a covert form of taxation, depriving people of the freedom to spend, or not spend, as they choose. The bill's supporters don't call it a tax, of course. But that doesn't change the fact that it is one.

Imagine if the government forced you to pay $3,600 per year to the U.S. Treasury so Uncle Sam could subsidize insurance companies. You'd call it a tax, right?

Well, suppose the government told you to bypass the U.S. Treasury and write your check directly to a private insurance company. It would still be a tax. You'd still be out $3,600. The only thing that would change is the payee's name on the check. You are forced by law to write that check.

Nevertheless, because Obamacare forces individuals to write checks to insurance companies—and not the U.S. Treasury—the government does not categorize the individual mandate as a tax.

There's an old joke that if you paint an elephant's toenails red, you can hide it in the strawberry patch. Well, supporters of Obamacare have attempted to hide this elephant-sized tax with a similarly absurd tactic.

It's very simple. If the government forces you to pay money, it's a tax—regardless of whose name is on the check.

CONSTITUTIONALLY CHALLENGED

Obamacare justifies the individual mandate under the federal government's power to regulate commerce.

The bill states that the individual mandate "regulates activity that is commercial and economic in nature: economic and financial decisions about how and when health care is paid for, and when health insurance is purchased."[6]

And yet the power to regulate commerce has never been interpreted in this way.

As Georgetown constitutional law professor Randy E. Barnett wrote, "The [Supreme] Court has never upheld a requirement that individuals who are doing nothing *must* engage in economic activity by entering into a contractual relationship with a private company."[7]

Indeed, if people refuse to buy insurance, isn't that the exact opposite of commerce? It's hard to see how the federal government can justify a mandate on the grounds that refusing to buy something is a form of commercial activity.

As of May 2010, at least twenty state attorneys general and governors were challenging the individual mandate on constitutional grounds, arguing that the federal government has overstepped its bounds.[8] Notably, the National Federation of Independent Business, which has 350,000 members, has also joined the general lawsuit.[9]

House Speaker Nancy Pelosi has described this challenge as "frivolous." And HHS Secretary Kathleen Sebelius has said it has "more to do with politics than policy." The Obama Justice Department, however, seems to be having a tough time preparing for its case. In late May 2010, Justice officials asked for a one-month extension. Judge Roger Vinson, the federal judge hearing the suit in Florida district court, denied the request.[10]

The following month, the Justice Department filed a motion to have the case dropped altogether. Obama insisted during the health care debate that the individual mandate was not a "tax" (see above). The Justice Department, in its dismissal motion, defends the mandate under the power of Congress to "tax and spend."

When the constitutionality of the individual mandate comes up for Supreme Court review, as it almost certainly will, there's a good chance that the mandate will be struck down.

A FAILED EXPERIMENT

It should come as no surprise that people resist when told to pay up.

Well before Obamacare was passed, we had an example of how the individual mandate works in practice, and it wasn't pretty. Massachusetts passed a law in April 2006 mandating insurance coverage by one of two means: Either employers with eleven or more fulltime employees had to provide insurance or pay a fine;[11] or individuals had to buy it themselves, on pain of losing their income tax deduction.

Early reports on the Massachusetts plan claimed the state had managed to sign up 442,000 more people for health insurance. The reality was that 80,000 of these were simply put on Medicaid, and 176,000 more joined taxpayer-subsidized plans.

Even those who enrolled in the state's subsidized Commonwealth Care program had problems. As of 2009, 20 percent of them were having a hard time finding a doctor because of the low reimbursement rates the program paid to providers.

Meanwhile, plans available to private buyers were so unaffordable that, by the end of 2007, 62,000 people had been exempted from the individual mandate.

In total, 168,000 adults still remained without health insurance.[12] More than half of them, 97,000, had not bought insurance even though they could afford a policy, according to the state Department of Revenue.[13] Of those, 86,000 paid the penalty, and 11,000 appealed it.[14]

At the same time, costs to both the state and individuals were rising rapidly.

Between 2007 and 2009, the maximum penalty for not having insurance jumped from $219 to $1,068.[15]

Premiums for the state's unsubsidized Commonwealth Choice program were expected to increase by an average of 5 percent in 2009, while government payments toward premiums in Commonwealth Care were expected to increase by an average of 9.4 percent.[16]

The state's costs exploded, requiring tax hikes and sizable transfers from the federal government.

This is the kind of debacle Obamacare has now brought to the rest of the nation.

COMPOUNDING THE PROBLEM

As we've seen in Massachusetts, an individual mandate neither brings down costs nor leads to universal coverage. But two policies implemented in Massachusetts in 2006, and now rolling out across the country, make the problem worse.

The first is "guaranteed issue."

A handful of states have had a guaranteed-issue provision in place for years. It requires insurers to offer coverage to any and all would-be customers, regardless of preexisting conditions.

This has a clear-cut psychological effect. If customers know that insurance could cost more once they contract an illness, there's an incentive for them to buy it while they're still healthy. But if they know it will cost the same even after they get sick, there's no downside to waiting to subscribe.

The result is that the customer base for any given provider is weighted heavily towards the sick.

The second policy is known as "community rating." That's when insurers must offer the same premium to all customers, regardless of their age or health.

Obamacare advocates claim that community rating will lower the cost for customers with severe health problems. What they don't mention is that this policy will force insurance companies to raise premiums for everyone else.

In effect, companies average out the risk so high-risk patients pay less than they otherwise would, while the much greater number of low-risk patients pay more.

By raising costs for the latter group, community rating reinforces the effect of guaranteed issue—giving even more incentive for healthy people to wait until they are sick to buy insurance.

New York instituted a health care policy with these two mandates back in 1993. The results were clear within just a few years.

As economics columnist Steven Malanga observed, before the 1993 reforms went into effect, about 752,000 residents were buying health insurance themselves. After the reforms, premiums immediately began to skyrocket, and New York's individual market all but disappeared, quickly shrinking by 95 percent to a mere 34,000 buyers.

By 1997, the ranks of the uninsured in New York had risen to 20 percent of the population.[17] A study by the Manhattan Institute calculated that the Empire State's mandates increased the cost of health premiums by 42 percent.[18]

Wary of repeating New York's mistake, Massachusetts tried to stop people from fleeing the market with the individual mandate. But as we've seen, a mandate still doesn't convince everyone to join. And since guaranteed issue and community rating both drive up premiums, the incentive to pay the fine rather than buy insurance will only increase over time.

It's starting to happen already.

The *Boston Globe* reported that in 2009, 936 people signed up for coverage with Blue Cross Blue Shield of Massachusetts for three months or less—and ran up claims of more than $1,000 per month while in the system.[19]

While insured, their medical spending was more than four times the average for consumers who retained coverage over a long period. The short-term members typically paid about $400 a month for coverage, but claimed, on average, more than $2,200 a month. The *Globe* estimated that the price tag for such temporary subscribers ran into the millions of dollars over two years.[20]

At another insurer, Harvard Pilgrim, between April 2008 and March 2009, about 40 percent of new customers stayed on the rolls for fewer than five months and incurred, on average, costs that were 600 percent higher than what the company would have otherwise expected.[21]

When Obamacare goes into effect nationwide, we can expect people to start gaming the system on a massive scale. We can only guess what the cost of that will be.

THE BATTLE OVER PREMIUMS

In 2009, three of the largest four insurers in Massachusetts—Blue Cross Blue Shield, Tufts Health Plan, and Fallon Community Health, all non-profits—posted operating losses.[22] Naturally, as the cost of doing business rose, they and other insurers wanted to raise prices.

To help staunch the losses, insurers asked regulators for permission to increase rates for small-business plans,[23] which cover about 800,000 residents.[24]

In April 2010, Massachusetts Governor Deval Patrick, kicking off his reelection campaign, declared that regulators would reject about 90 percent of the increases insurers had asked for.[25] Insurers balked and went to Boston superior court, where in an emergency suit they argued that the unexpected capping of rates would likely result in another $100 million in collective losses—and even threaten to put the companies out of business.

They also stopped selling policies. State officials promptly demanded that the insurers resume offering quotes at rates that were a year old. So just four years after passage, Massachusetts' reform had the government ordering companies to do business.

The battle continued through the spring. Four of the largest insurers posted losses of $150 million for the first quarter of 2010. In April, the state's Division of Insurance blocked insurers from significantly raising premiums. In May, the state senate passed a measure expanding the authority regulators had over insurance premiums.[26]

So insurance companies were barred from increasing rates. Not surprisingly, they announced that they needed to cut payments to hospitals and large group practices.[27] Hospital executives then responded by saying that many hospitals could not withstand rate freezes or reductions, since the state had cut Medicaid payments, and the federal government was likely to reduce Medicare payments under federal health reform.[28]

In the meantime, Bay State Insurance proposed that the government stop paying health care providers for each procedure, and instead compensate provider networks with a flat fee per patient. This kind of system of global payments, or "capitation," encourages provider groups to skimp on care as they get to profit from money not spent treating patients.[29]

There is also a bill in the Massachusetts legislature—Senate bill 2170, "An Act Relative to an Affordable Health Plan"—which, if passed, would require physicians to see Medicaid patients under threat of loss of licensure.

So let's review: By the middle of 2010, both insurers and hospitals faced the possibility of going out of business if they didn't raise rates. Patients faced the possibility of worse care under a global payment system. Plus, Massachusetts residents were looking at an ongoing rise in premiums, averaging 7.5 percent a year since 2000[30]—and were now required by the state to buy health insurance.

Surely, all this government coercion must have saved money for Massachusetts taxpayers, right?

Not so.

State Treasurer Timothy P. Cahill has called the Massachusetts program a "fiscal train wreck."[31] Writing in the *Wall Street Journal* in March 2010, Cahill observed that when the program was adopted in 2006, the universal coverage scheme was projected to cost taxpayers $880 million a year. By 2010 total costs had exceeded $4 billion,[32] more than 11 times the projection.[33]

If it weren't for injections of federal money, the state would have already been broke. As Cahill wrote, "Who will bail America out if we implement a similar program?"

Good question.

NOT JUST THE BAY STATE

While Massachusetts may stand out as a shining example of how not to overhaul health care, there are other state-level models that could have served as guideposts for federal policy makers.

In the 1990s, eight states—Kentucky, Maine, Massachusetts, New Hampshire, New Jersey, New York, Vermont, and Washington—implemented community rating and guaranteed issue.[34] The Council for Affordable Health Insurance studied the ugly results about a decade later, in 2005.

Consider what they found in New Jersey. Between 1992, when the legislation passed, and 2005, the state saw a 40 to 50 percent decline in insurance coverage.

Premiums also went up. Aetna's monthly premiums for one of its family plans increased 683 percent, from $769 in 1994 to $6,025 in 2005, or a stunning $72,300 a year. Other companies were, by 2005, offering similar rates; at New Jersey Blue Cross Blue Shield, a family policy cost $89,424 a year.[35]

The data were similar around the country. Between 1994 and 2003, in all eight states that implemented these programs, the share of the population covered by individual health insurance fell dramatically.

Insurance companies packed up and left. For example, forty-five insurers fled Kentucky between 1994 and 1997.

Meanwhile, premiums in all eight states soared.[36]

In 2003, Maine tried to mend matters by passing its Dirigo Health plan, centered on a subsidized insurance scheme called DirigoChoice. Unfortunately it didn't scrap guaranteed issue or community rating.[37]

Democratic Governor John Baldacci claimed that Dirigo Health would cover all of the state's 128,000 uninsured Mainers within five years.[38]

Instead, at its enrollment peak in 2006, DirigoChoice covered a total of 15,000 people.

The sickest, most expensive customers had taken advantage of DirigoChoice, but this heavily tilted the insurance pool and raised costs. As premiums rose, it became unappealing to healthier would-be subscribers, tilting the pool even more. In the end, few low-income Mainers could afford the premiums, even at subsidized rates.[39]

THE COMING FAILURE

All signs point to the likely failure of Obamacare, which includes many of the most problematic policies that we've seen at the state level. Possibly the most glaring among them is the individual mandate.

Some have argued that without an individual mandate, few healthy people would buy coverage, causing insurers to raise premiums. That may be true—but only because the individual mandate is tied up with community rating and guaranteed issue.

With insurers barred from adjusting premiums based on customers' risk factors, and forced to take all comers at all times, many Americans will simply game the system.

With weak fines for failure to obtain coverage, healthy people will have a strong motivation to save money by not purchasing insurance. If they get sick, they can buy it for the same price as they could if they were healthy. As a result, insurers will be forced to raise rates on everyone.

Americans, required by law to buy insurance, will find themselves doing so in a marketplace of ever-higher prices.

In short, by 2014, when many of the provisions take effect, we'll be heading into a "fiscal train wreck" of the kind seen in Massachusetts. Only this time, there won't be anyone to bail us out.

CHAPTER 9

MINIMUM COVERAGE, MAXIMUM COST

Imagine if the United States government passed a law declaring, "No person shall be allowed to purchase a computer unless it's manufactured by Sony or Samsung. The computer must come with a Bluetooth mouse and keyboard, surround-sound speakers, and a 27-inch widescreen LCD monitor. It must be equipped with an Intel Core 2 Quad processor, 32 gigabytes of RAM, and at least two terabytes of hard drive space. Effective immediately, laptops are prohibited."

Obviously, such a policy would be incredibly elitist—only the wealthy would be able to afford such tricked-out desktops, and poor people would be forced to go without personal computers.

This may sound like a far-fetched scenario, but in the lunatic world of health care, government regulations that dictate what people can and can't buy are commonplace. In fact, these "mandates" are a primary reason many Americans can't afford health insurance today.

Take the typical healthy 25-year-old male discussed in chapter 7, who has just entered the workforce. He might very well decide that $300 a month for health insurance—a typical rate for a single person—isn't worth it for the few medical services he needs.

It would be a monumental waste of money for him to pay $3,600 a year so that he can be 80 percent covered for regular visits to the doctor's office, especially considering he hasn't been to the doctor in years.

He doesn't need a pricey policy covering unlimited checkups and everything from *in vitro* fertilization to drug abuse counseling. All he needs is "catastrophic" coverage to protect him in the off-chance something terrible happens, like getting hit by a bus or diagnosed with cancer.

Such sensible policies, however, are difficult to find because of government mandates. Every state mandates that insurers provide a number of benefits. In some states, these mandates are so onerous that they effectively prohibit insurers from tailoring policies for the young and healthy.

Under Obamacare, this problem is made even worse, because it forbids, by federal law, insurers from offering inexpensive, bare-bones policies. It does so under a multitude of "minimum coverage standards."

WHY MANDATES DON'T MAKE SENSE

These mandates don't just cover essential services, like emergency room visits.

Since 2000, at the state level, insurers have been required to cover hearing aids, hormone replacement therapy, and reimbursement for clinical trial participation.[1] Many mandates—like massage therapy—are hardly critical components of a good insurance policy. They exist because special-interest groups—like chiropractors and addiction counselors—have lobbied lawmakers to add their particular service to the list of required benefits.

In 1979, there were only 252 mandates in place in the states—an average of five per state.[2] By 2009, there were 2,133 mandates—an average of forty-two per state.[3]

Very few of us will ever require breast reduction surgery. But that procedure is required in several states.

Most of us get our diet advice from books, magazines, and the Internet. But some states force insurers to make dieticians available for one-on-one counseling. For those who ignore diet advice, some states even cover "morbid obesity treatment."

This is just the tip of the iceberg. Alternative therapies like acupuncture are mandated in some places. Treatments used by a small percentage of the population, like hormone replacement therapy for some menopause-aged women, or *in vitro* fertilization for couples who can't conceive, are required for everyone in some states.

You might not be sexually active, but most states require insurers to cover contraceptives. Some states mandate marriage therapy. A few states even require insurers to pay for athletic trainers![4]

Needless to say, forcing every insurance plan to cover such a broad range of conditions and treatments, whether a customer wants them covered or not, drives up insurers' costs. That in turn drives up premiums.

In 2004, three economists from the Council of Economic Advisers studied the effects of state mandates on the individual health insurance market. Their findings? "Mandated benefits raise the expected price of an individual policy by approximately 0.4 percent per mandate. For family policies the increase is approximately 0.5 percent per mandate."[5]

With the number of mandates ranging from thirteen (in Idaho) to seventy (in Rhode Island), these so-called "benefits" come at a high cost.[6]

Mandates drive up the cost of insurance for Idahoans by 2.4 percent, while mandate-heavy Rhode Islanders shoulder premiums 18.6 percent higher than they otherwise might be.[7]

In total, benefit mandates force premiums up by 10.5 percent in the average state, according to a 2010 study by Pacific Research Institute scholar Benjamin Zycher.[8] That translates to an additional $1,294 tacked on to the average policy for a family that gets its coverage through an employer.[9] The average self-employed individual who purchases coverage for himself must shell out an extra $299 a year to pay for mandated benefits he may never use.

Other studies have reached similar conclusions. The Council for Affordable Health Insurance has found that mandated benefits increase the cost of basic health coverage by as much as 50 percent.[10]

THE MANDATES OF OBAMACARE

While campaigning for his legislation, President Obama promised over and over again that his plan would cut the cost of a typical family's insurance premium. "If you like your current health insurance, nothing changes, except your costs will go down."

His new Act, though, piles scores of new benefit mandates on top of the state ones. So common sense dictates that our insurance costs will rise. Let's take a look at the mandates Obamacare imposes.

For starters, it mandates that all insurance policies not only cover preventative care, but cover it completely—there can be no cost-sharing. In other words, insurers can no longer even charge *co-payments* for preventative care. Seeing your doctor for a routine physical will still cost money, of course, so this mandate simply means that such costs will be hidden in your insurance premium.[11]

There are many more mandates included in the new state-run health insurance exchanges—the one-stop health insurance shopping malls where consumers who are not offered insurance through their employers—or who can't afford that coverage—will be able to purchase insurance.

Besides covering typical emergency services and hospitalization, policies on the exchanges will have to cover maternity care and pediatric services—even for folks who are single and childless, and even for those who can't conceive. Substance abuse services and rehab coverage are also mandated on the exchanges—even for non-alcohol consuming Mormons.[12]

These mandates are just the beginning—the legislation explicitly states that insurance plans on the exchanges "shall include at least the following." And just as state mandates grew from 252 to 2,133 over three decades, we can now expect the same exponential growth in federal mandates.

Keep in mind that the exchanges are supposedly for people who are unable to afford the insurance provided by their employer. How such people will afford insurance with all these bells and whistles is unclear.

Obamacare also prohibits annual and lifetime limits on insurance coverage effective September 23, 2010. These limits have, in the past, allowed some people to keep their health care costs down; they agree that they can bill their insurers only so much money—often around $1 or $2 million—and in exchange are offered lower premiums. Such policies are now illegal.[13]

Obamacare doesn't just redefine insurance—it also redefines childhood. Effective September 23, 2010, insurers that provide coverage of dependents must now cover those dependents until they're twenty-six years old.[14]

Obamacare advocates have trumpeted the fact that the bill prohibits insurance companies from rescinding coverage from those who become sick. This, however, was *already illegal*. Federal regulations have prohibited insurers from raising a sick person's premiums since 1997. No matter how sick a patient gets, an insurance company can't drop an existing customer's policy or refuse to renew it—provided that the person was truthful on the insurance application and still lives in the state where the policy was issued.[15] Moreover, state health commissioners across the country were already policing such behavior to make sure insurance companies didn't drop sick clients.

Bottom line: Health care is highly personal. We all have different needs. Some of us are young and healthy and don't use the system much. Some of us are aging and see our doctors regularly. We don't use the same services, so why should we pay for the same services?

None of us would buy a pair of pants that said "one size fits all" on the label. Why are we forced to buy "one size fits all" health insurance?

CHAPTER 10

DOUBLING DOWN ON A BAD SYSTEM

merican health insurance has been tied to employment ever since the implementation of wage controls during the Second World War. Today, when a company provides insurance to its workers, both the employer and its employees receive a tax write-off. If those same employees tried to purchase coverage independently, they would be penalized by the tax code.

As a result, more than 60 percent of Americans are now covered by health insurance that is paid, in part or in full, by an employer.[1] This employer-based system creates all kinds of market distortions, and has utterly failed to keep health care spending under control.

Unfortunately, Obamacare does nothing to mend this broken system. Instead, it doubles down on it by heavily fining companies that don't provide insurance. In short, Obamacare embeds employer-based coverage even deeper into American health care.

MAKING A BAD SYSTEM WORSE

American health care has become an almost exclusively "third-party" based system, in that someone else is paying the bill. For Americans not covered by Medicare or Medicaid, that "someone" is usually their employer who has contracted with an insurance company to provide coverage.

When insurance premiums are subsidized by a person's company, health care appears to be a lot cheaper than it really is, and employees are indirectly encouraged to take advantage of as much "health care" as possible, regardless of its cost.

Needless to say, this drives up costs for the insurance companies, who in turn raise prices.

In this system, the insurance company, not the patient, is the doctor's customer. As a result, even dedicated providers have an incentive to skimp on service and over-bill for their work.

If doctors had to compete for customers, they would face pressure to lower prices. But no such competition exists. Customers don't shop around because their coverage is provided through a third-party. Patients have no idea—and no incentive to care—what services actually cost.

Insurers, meanwhile, have no reason to worry about consumer complaints, since the employers, not the patients, are their customers. That may account for the frustration so many of us feel when dealing with our insurance companies, with their incomprehensible rule books and interminable telephone wait times. If insurers had to compete for our business, the customer experience would count.

In short, we've created a system in which costs rise steadily, while patients receive inferior care.

NEW PENALTIES, MORE UNEMPLOYMENT

Obamacare reinforces this employer-based system.

To begin with, the new legislation punishes medium-to-large companies that don't cover their workers.

As of 2014, employers with fifty or more full-time employees will face the possibility of a fine if they don't provide health insurance. Moreover, if their employees enroll on their own in a "qualified" insurance plan and are eligible for a subsidy (specifically, a premium tax credit or cost-sharing reduction) from the federal government, then the company must pay a monthly fine of $167 *per* employee ($2,000 a year). Bizarrely, it doesn't matter how many employees receive federal assistance, the fine is applied against the employer for *every* full-time employee after the first thirty, so an employer of fifty employees could be hit be with a $40,000 fine.[2]

Companies with more than fifty employees who *do* offer health insurance can still be fined if one or more of their employees chooses to enroll in a federally subsidized plan. So long as the company's plan pays less than 60 percent of the cost of benefits, or if the premiums cost the worker more than 9.5 percent of his or her household income, the company can be fined.[3]

In such cases, the employer must pay a penalty of $250 a month (or $3,000 a year) for each employee receiving a premium credit. This penalty cannot exceed $167 per month (or $2,000 per year) for all the companies' full-time employees.

Sadly, these new rules will fall most heavily on companies that hire lower-income workers, who are disproportionately non-whites, high-school dropouts, and women. That's because, as a percentage of salary, the per-worker cost of providing health insurance is much higher for low-income workers than it is for high-income workers.

The Congressional Budget Office estimates that by 2016, the cost of an employer-sponsored plan covering 70 percent of health expenses will be $15,200 for a family.[4]

If an employer wants to hire a $300,000-a-year lawyer, then paying an extra $15,200 in health insurance isn't a big deal. It's just a 5 percent premium. But if that employer wants to hire a $24,000-a-year receptionist, the health insurance policy now makes that receptionist 63 percent more expensive. The employer might decide that the new receptionist isn't worth the money.

Lower-skilled workers compete for jobs with higher-skilled workers by charging less. Obamacare dampens this competitive advantage by making it more expensive, relatively speaking, to hire low-skilled workers—which, in turn, makes them less attractive to potential employers.

PUTTING BUSINESSES OUT OF BUSINESS

Why does Obamacare penalize companies with more than forty-nine employees?

Nobody knows.

But obviously this arbitrary threshold will have an equally arbitrary and unintended consequence, distorting the market, and ultimately leading to a loss of jobs, encouraging companies to keep their payrolls under fifty full-time employees, unless they want to face a potential fine of $40,000.[5]

Instead of expanding, businesses will likely rely more on independent contractors or reduce wages so they can cover health insurance premiums, or export jobs overseas. Many small and medium-size businesses on tight margins will simply be crushed.

It's already happening.

Doug Newman, owner of Newman Concrete Services in Richmond, Maine, had seen his workforce shrink from 125 to 25 during the recent recession. He told the Associated Press at the end of March 2010 that in order to avoid the mandate, he might only hire back 25 or fewer workers, just a quarter of the number he let go. That's because if he passes the 49-employee mark, he'll no longer be exempt from penalties.[6]

The Associated Press also reported the story of Don Day, who owns two restaurants, a hotel, and several retail shops in McKinney, Texas. At the time the bill was passed, he employed 125 workers, but only offered health care to a few key players. Under the new bill, he'll have to cover everyone. Adding a few hundred dollars a month per employee could cost him hundreds of thousands of dollars a year—which he says he can't afford.

As he told the Associated Press, "A lot of small businesses are going to go out of business."[7]

UNINTENDED CONSEQUENCES

The bill does include a few tax credits that are supposed to help small businesses.

Employers with fewer than twenty-five employees and average wages of less than $40,000 a year get a credit of up to 35 percent of the employer's contribution, but only from 2010 through 2013. And smaller companies with a lower average wage can get a tax credit of up to 50 percent of the employer's contribution, beginning in 2014.[8]

In both cases, the credit gets smaller and smaller as the size of the company and average pay rise. As economists Devon Herrick and Pamela Villarreal of the National Center for Policy Analysis have pointed out, this penalizes companies for raising average pay and hiring additional workers.

"Instead of hiring ditch diggers and giving each one a shovel, an employer might buy a backhoe and hire a more highly skilled operator," they write. "An unintended consequence of the law is that some low wage workers will be unemployed who otherwise would not be."[9]

One in ten businesses plans on restricting employment to compensate for the increased costs caused by Obamacare, according to a May 2010 survey conducted by the consulting firm Towers Watson. And 74 percent of firms surveyed plan to pass the law's higher costs on to their employees by changing plan options, restricting eligibility, or increasing deductibles or co-pays.

The net result: low-skilled workers lose, big time, as wages fall, businesses close, and jobs disappear.

MISSED OPPORTUNITIES

With the passage of Obamacare, our legislators missed an enormous opportunity to fix one of the most unfair aspects of our health care system: the way it penalizes the self-employed.

In the United States, individuals who work for themselves must pay for health insurance using post-tax earnings. Those who are employed by big companies are able to use pre-tax earnings to pay for the same coverage.

Under our current tax code, there are effectively two categories of consumers, and those employed by large companies receive preferential treatment.

This discourages people from starting businesses. Obamacare punishes the very entrepreneurs who drive America's economic growth. It gives preferential treatment to the employee who relies on a corporate pay check, over an independent entrepreneur who works for himself.

Obamacare expanded one of the worse aspects of American health care, the third party system, meaning costs will be driven up and businesses will go under.

CHAPTER 11

FEWER CHOICES, LESS COMPETITION

Government has been pushing "managed competition" in health care for a long time. In 1959, Congress created the Federal Employees Health Benefits (FEHB) Program to provide health insurance to government workers and their families.[1] Rather than offer a single government-run health plan, the program allowed employees to pick from a variety of private insurance plans pre-screened by the federal Office of Personnel Management (OPM).

While different plans were allowed to compete by charging different rates and offering slightly different benefits, the competition would be "managed" by the government. All plans were required to operate under very strict mandates.[2]

Within just a few years, some policy wonks started pushing the FEHB as a model for national health insurance.[3] Fast forward to the 1990s, and the phrase "managed competition" appeared in President Bill Clinton's health policy speeches over and over again,[4] with FEHB as the model.[5]

Indeed, the centerpiece of Clinton's reform plan required that all insurers offer the same basic benefit package and the same patient cost-sharing options.

The theory, at the time, was that this reform would increase competition by persuading consumers to ignore benefits and focus solely on premiums and quality.[6]

Americans didn't buy it.

But among folks who prefer the bureaucratic hand to the invisible one, the push for managed competition didn't go away. During the 2008 presidential campaign, then-Senator Obama called for the creation of a single, regulated marketplace for health insurance called a "national health insurance exchange."[7]

In a slightly different format, that vision became law when President Obama signed the health reform bill.

Under Obamacare, the government will provide states with start-up funding to establish what will be called "American Health Benefit Exchanges." These state-run exchanges will approve, regulate, and broker insurance plans for people not covered through their employers. They're supposed to be functioning by 2014.[8]

Proponents claim these exchanges will be convenient, one-stop health insurance shopping malls. More preposterously, they say the exchanges will stoke competition by giving consumers a single outlet where they can compare the benefits and prices of different plans.

In reality, the exchanges are far more likely to suppress competition than encourage it.

Relying on the government to oversee market competition is like paying an alcoholic to administer sobriety checkpoints. Markets work best when the government minimizes regulation.

Think of televisions, bikes, books, or fresh produce. With just about every consumer product, there are multiple, thriving markets. Congress didn't have to pass complex laws authorizing bureaucrats to design these markets. These markets evolved through the ongoing interplay between sellers and buyers.

If there's a lack of competition in today's health insurance market, it's *because of* government interference.

If Obama and his allies in Congress had truly wanted to create a competitive national market for health insurance, they could have changed the federal tax code to allow individuals to purchase health insurance with pre-tax dollars, just like large employers can. Or they could have allowed Americans to purchase health insurance across state lines. Or they could have lifted the numerous mandates on insurance policies instead of increasing them.

COMMAND AND CONTROL

Despite the bill's 2,409 pages of legalese, it's still not clear what the exchanges will look like on January 1, 2014.

Much of the uncertainty lies in the sheer number of exchanges. While some states might choose to open actual stores in local shopping malls, others may try to keep everything on the Internet. States will be required to offer assistance over the telephone and through a website.[9]

With fifty states offering fifty different exchanges, there are bound to be drastic differences in how each functions. However they are structured, though, one thing is certain—the exchanges will be the vehicles through which the government dramatically expands its control over the health care system.

Just as the Office of Personnel Management prescreens private insurance plans before accepting them into the Federal Employees Health Benefits (FEHB) Program, each state-based American Health Benefit Exchange will make certain that all available policies meet both state and federal mandates.

If an insurance plan is especially generous, it can win a "platinum" rating from the state-based exchanges.

The exchanges will also offer gold, silver, and bronze plans. Perhaps the congressional staffers who drafted this section of the bill spent February 2010 watching the Olympics. Their time would have been better spent studying how insurance mandates actually work, because mandated benefits can increase the cost of basic health coverage by as much as 50 percent.[10]

Some lawmakers would like to go so far as to dictate how much insurers are allowed to charge for coverage. Senator Dianne Feinstein introduced a bill that would give the Secretary of Health and Human Services the freedom to reject "any rate increase found to be unreasonable." President Obama entertained a similar proposal in an early version of his health care plan. And Senator Tom Harkin reintroduced the idea in April 2010.[11]

Thankfully, the exchanges won't be allowed to set prices, but they will be able to ask insurance companies to justify any premium hikes. If the answer isn't satisfactory, an exchange can simply cite price as a reason to drop that particular insurance plan.

Technically, folks in the individual and small group market will still be able to purchase health coverage outside the exchanges after 2014. But insurers would be required to charge the same rates outside the exchanges as they do inside.

Put simply, the exchanges will drive up the price of insurance and reduce consumer choice.

Shockingly, the people who helped design the bill admitted that this was part of their plan. According to Judy Solomon of the Obama-friendly Center on Budget and Policy Priorities, in order to be effective, "the exchanges should limit the number and variety of plans."[12]

No wonder early versions of this section of the bill actually would have created a "Health Choices Commissioner."[13]

AN INEFFECTIVE STOPGAP

Because most of these exchanges won't be up and running until 2014, Obamacare allocates $5 billion to create a temporary network of high-risk pools to help provide "immediate access to insurance" for people with preexisting conditions who have been uninsured for at least six months.[14] In 2014, these people will be transferred to the exchanges.

In reality, though, Obamacare will actually *take coverage away* from many of these people over the next few years.

Under the bill, states were asked to establish and administer these high-risk pools on their own. Eighteen states refused, leaving the federal government to do the work.[15] Most of the other states—the majority of which already have their own high-risk pools—volunteered to set these new pools up.

The new high-risk pools will exist parallel to the old pools. Most of the old pools, though, are quite expensive—often costing twice as much as standard insurance policies.[16] Since Obamacare's pools will be much cheaper, these new pools will have to match the standard insurance prices in the states they're offered. So folks with preexisting conditions will have a financial incentive to switch to the new pools.

But there's a catch. To qualify for these new high-risk pools, individuals must be uninsured for at least six months. So folks with preexisting conditions who currently receive health coverage through a state-based high-risk pool will face a terrible choice—either drop their existing insurance policy for six months and hope for the best, or stick with their existing plan even though there's now a much cheaper option.

This restriction was purposeful. As the AARP's John Rother explained, "To switch over all those people would have definitely boosted the cost, and Congress was looking for ways to minimize it."[17]

Shortchanging the states also minimized the cost of these new pools. According to Richard Foster, chief actuary of the Centers for Medicare and Medicaid Services, the $5 billion set aside by Congress to create these pools will likely run out in

2011 or 2012. As a result, states that signed up to administer these new pools will end up shouldering the full cost of running them for about two full years.[18]

Many believe that the situation will be even worse. In late May 2010, the Center for Studying Health System Change issued a report which concluded that even though as many as 5.6 to 7 million Americans may qualify for the temporary high risk pools, there's only enough funding to cover about 200,000 people annually.[19]

SETTING THE STAGE FOR A GOVERNMENT TAKEOVER

Throughout the health care debate, President Obama and liberal members of Congress called for the creation of a government-run insurance plan to "compete" with private firms. While their effort was unsuccessful, they haven't given up.

At a health care panel in April 2010, Democrat Congressman Henry Waxman of California—the chairman of the House Energy and Commerce Committee—told attendees that if the exchanges failed to foster competition and lower costs, he would begin pushing for a "public option"—in other words, government-run health care.

The Congressional Budget Office already predicts price hikes of 10 to 13 percent[20] thanks to Obamacare. Given that insurance premiums are almost certain to rise rapidly within the exchanges, a push for a public option (government-provided health insurance) is likely to come sooner rather than later.

By drawing on taxpayer dollars, this public option would be able to out-price almost every private insurer in the country. Unable to compete, private insurers would be "crowded out," leaving Americans with just one choice: a government-operated health care plan that brings the entire health sector under government control. During the health care debate, The Lewin Group, a respected health care consulting firm, estimated that 119 million Americans would lose their employer-based coverage if Congress were to create such a federal alternative to private insurance.

More choice and more competition? Hardly.

CHAPTER 12

THE ROAD
TO RATIONING

While many elements of Obamacare are going to be phased in over ten years, one component got a big head start. In the economic stimulus package, which was passed in 2009,[1] Congress allocated $1.1 billion over two years to fund a little-known scholarly field called Comparative Effectiveness Research, or CER.

When Obamacare passed the following year, it terminated the previous effort and created a whole new organization—the Patient-Centered Outcomes Research Institute—to conduct studies in the area of CER.[2]

So what exactly is Comparative Effectiveness Research?

As the words suggest, it's research that compares the effectiveness of different medical treatments—surgery, pharmaceuticals, biologics, and other medical therapies—to see how they stack up against each other.

When employed properly, CER arms doctors and patients with information on various options so they can choose the best treatment for any medical circumstance.

Unfortunately, CER is often misused. When governments employ CER, they don't just compare the efficacy of various treatments, they also compare costs. They use those cost comparisons to determine which treatments are covered under government health care programs.

If you're dying from a heart attack, there's a big difference between the most *medically effective* treatment and the most *cost-effective* treatment. One will save your life; the other will save money for the government.

While proponents argue that CER can save taxpayer money, what they neglect to say is that CER saves money by empowering the government to deny expensive procedures and treatments. In fact, many governments use CER to justify rationing.

RATIONING IN ACTION—NOT SO NICE

There could be no better example of how CER is used to justify rationing than in the United Kingdom. The country's health care system is run by a publicly funded government agency called the National Health Service (NHS).

The NHS routinely relies on CER to hold down costs.

Here's how the process works: An organization within the NHS called the National Institute for Health and Clinical Effectiveness (NICE) analyzes CER studies, then makes recommendations to the NHS about what treatments should be covered under Britain's national health care plan.

NICE arrives at its decisions by evaluating treatments based on estimates of cost and how long those treatments will extend a patient's life. It uses a particularly distasteful measure known as a Quality Adjusted Life Year (QALY) to stick a numeric value on one year of a person's life. The healthier you are, the higher the number.

Quality of life, of course, is fairly subjective, especially when it's yours, or a loved one's.

Quick! Which is a better use of taxpayer money: 1) helping a terminal pancreatic cancer patient live for six extra months in moderate pain; or 2) helping a patient live for twelve months with reduced mobility from rheumatoid arthritis?

Agencies like NICE ask—and answer—these questions all the time.

NICE looks at how long a patient is likely to live with—and without—a given treatment, plus the success rate and cost of that treatment. If you happen to be a patient in desperate need of a life-saving medicine, your fate depends on how NICE crunches the numbers.

In short, NICE puts a dollar value on human life. According to a BBC analysis, if a treatment costs more than $45,000 per patient per year of added life, NICE will likely recommend that the treatment not be covered.[3]

NICE frequently makes headlines for unpopular decisions about what drugs should be available to UK citizens.

In 2006, NICE refused to recommend the breakthrough chemotherapy drug Alimta for the treatment of mesothelioma, a generally fatal cancer associated with asbestos exposure. Amid public backlash, NICE eventually reversed its decision.[4]

In 2007, and again in 2008, NICE refused to approve abatacept, a drug sold in the United States under the brand-name Orencia for the treatment of rheumatoid arthritis. Abatacept is one of the only drugs clinically proven to improve severe rheumatoid arthritis. It also represents a last chance for patients to lead pain-free lives when other treatments have failed them. Yet NICE decided that the benefits of the drug could not be justified at $14,000 per patient per year.[5]

In 2008, NICE made a similar decision about the lung cancer drug Tarceva. Despite numerous studies showing that the drug significantly prolongs the life of cancer patients—and the unanimous endorsement of lung cancer specialists throughout the United Kingdom—NICE determined the drug was too expensive to cover.[6]

The fight over Tarceva was so contentious that it became a campaign issue in the United Kingdom.[7]

Ironically, despite the widespread public disapproval of the agency's tactics, Andrew Dillon, NICE's chief executive, was knighted in 2009.[8]

There are many more examples of NICE—and CER bodies in other countries—slowing the approval of cutting-edge medicines to keep costs down, from liver cancer treatments in the United Kingdom[9] to breast cancer drugs in New Zealand.[10]

COMING TO AMERICA

Unfortunately, with the passage of Obamacare, these unsavory cost-saving measures could now become part of America's health care woes.

In 2009, Americans got a preview of institutionalized CER when the U.S. Preventive Services Task Force, an advisory panel within HHS, decided to change its stance on mammograms. The Task Force recommended that women in their forties skip mammograms altogether, while women between fifty and seventy-four get mammograms every other year, rather than annually.[11]

How did the Task Force arrive at its decision? It made a financial calculation. It determined that in order to save a single life, 1,900 women in their forties would need to be screened. But only 1,300 screenings would be required to save a woman in her fifties. And it would take just 377 screenings of women in their sixties to save a life.[12]

Thus, as women grow older, it becomes increasingly cost effective to screen for breast cancer.

But does that mean that women in their forties shouldn't get mammograms? What if the life saved is yours—or your mother's, daughter's, or sister's? More important, are these the types of decisions that should be left to government? Do we really want bureaucrats deciding whose life is worth saving?

When the Task Force made its recommendation, people were outraged. There was an enormous public outcry—and the government quickly softened its stance. But it was a foreshadowing of what could happen if the government implements CER on a broad scale in this country.

Imagine if the Task Force's recommendations were used to determine what treatments would be covered under, say, Medicaid. That's exactly where CER could take us—not just with mammograms, but for every treatment and medical procedure under the sun.

RATIONING HEALTH CARE WILL STIFLE INNOVATION

Comparative Effectiveness Research could also lead to a stifling of innovation. It could force medical researchers to focus on developing treatments that are more likely to be approved, rather than treatments that are likely to save lives.

Pharmaceutical and medical device companies invest billions of dollars each year researching new treatments. It's a risky undertaking, with potentially huge rewards—which is why they're willing to put so much money into developing new cures.

That risk-reward calculation could change dramatically if CER is used to determine whether the government will pay for a given treatment. Using CER, the government would likely decide that a young person's life is worth more than an elderly person's life—driving research away from cures that benefit the elderly. After all, the cost of treatments for the elderly can't be amortized over as many years.

As a result, Alzheimer's research could take a back seat to, say, diabetes research. If the government drives such decisions, the "Death Panels" for seniors will become a reality. If nothing else, medical research, already skewed by government funding, will become frighteningly politicized.

SAVING MONEY OVER LIVES

CER is one of those policy ideas that is a wonderful *theoretical* tool. It can be used to educate and inform doctors and patients alike about various medical options. Unfortunately, it's often abused by governments to save money and deprive patients of critical treatments.

Obamacare takes the first steps toward institutionalizing CER in the United States by establishing the Patient-Centered Outcomes Research Institute, which will conduct research into the clinical effectiveness of various medical treatments—and report its findings to the government.

To be fair, the legislation does take steps to protect this country from the kind of rationing we've seen in the United Kingdom.

Although publicly funded, the Institute will be a non-profit corporation and not technically a government establishment. The legislation states that the Institute's research should not be used to deny treatments, and it bars the use of a "dollars-per-quality adjusted life year" to determine coverage.

Nevertheless, it would take only a few pen strokes to strike these protections and turn the Institute into an organization with a role similar to that of Britain's NICE. No one can predict the long-term outcome with certainty, but there's a terrifying risk that CER will be misused to lower health care quality by placing a greater emphasis on price than people. That's the inevitable direction of government-run health care.

CHAPTER 13

TAXING INNOVATION

According to the World Health Organization, "age related cataract is responsible for 48% of world blindness, which represents about 18 million people."[1] Fortunately, if you live in the United States, there are amazing technological cures for this fogging of the eye.

For instance, surgeons can actually remove the eye's natural, clouded lens and replace it with a clear, artificial one. Artificial lenses are just one of the many recent breakthroughs created by the medical device industry, which has developed artificial versions of everything from lower-back disks to hips and hearts.

Pharmaceutical companies have a similar story to tell. In just the past few years, they've developed medicines that drive cancer into remission, lower cholesterol, alleviate arthritis pain, and halt the progression of AIDS.

Unfortunately, the device and drug companies that develop these miracles of modern medicine will take a drubbing from Obamacare. The law forces them to pay extraordinary taxes—which, in turn, will either divert money away from new medical advances or be passed on to consumers in the form of higher prices.

BREAKDOWN OF TAXES

Let's start with pharmaceutical companies.

Under Obamacare, they'll have to pay $16.7 billion in new taxes through the end of the decade: $2.8 billion in 2012 to 2013; $3 billion in 2014 to 2016; $4 billion in 2014; $4.1 billion in 2018; and $2.8 billion in 2019.

Then they'll be taxed $2.8 billion annually every year after 2019. That's in addition to the taxes they already pay.

The industry will also make less on the drugs it provides to Medicaid patients. Obamacare imposes a massive discount of 23.1 percent on brand-name drugs used by Medicaid. Prior to Obamacare, this discount was 15.1 percent.

Medical device manufacturers also face a new tax.

They'll now pay an additional 2.3 percent excise tax on all their products, whether they're selling pacemakers, heart stents, wheelchairs, insulin pumps, CT scanners, or surgical gloves.

This tax is expected to channel about $2 billion annually away from this innovative industry. It will result in lots of extra money for government bureaucrats, and far less money for research into life-saving medical devices.

Of course, corporations don't pay taxes, individuals do. So these new taxes will ultimately be borne by consumers in the form of higher prices.

TOO MUCH OF THE PIE?

Many people think that these industries—especially the drug industry—are being singled out for extra taxes because they hog too much of the overall health care spending pie. But in fact, they account for a relatively small portion of health care spending given their outsized impact on improving the quality of patients' lives.

Americans spent an estimated $246 billion on prescription drugs in 2009.[2] That might sound like a lot, but medicine accounts for only 10 percent of total health spending.[3]

In fact, spending more money on medicine often means spending less money on hospital care and doctors' services, which make up a far greater percentage of our health care budget—$696.5 billion and $393.8 billion respectively.

Moreover, spending on medicine is rising less quickly than spending on other health care services.

Total health spending rose 6.1 percent in 2007—the year for which the journal *Health Affairs* did an in-depth report—but retail spending on drugs rose only 4.9 percent.

Meanwhile, hospital care spending rose 7.3 percent, and doctors' services rose 5.9 percent.[4]

LIPITOR IS CHEAPER THAN HEART SURGERY

Medical device and drug spending help keep these other costs down by obviating the need for prolonged hospital stays and expensive surgeries.

Illnesses like diabetes and heart disease demand regular treatment, sometimes for the rest of a patient's life. And, as the nation becomes older and possibly fatter, these ailments are becoming more common.

The prevalence of diabetes has nearly doubled in the last decade.[5] If the trend continues, one in three Americans will get the disease at some point;[6] and heart disease remains the nation's number one killer, killing one person every thirty-four seconds.[7]

Today, caring for people with chronic diseases accounts for about 85 percent of all U.S. health care spending.[8] One of the most effective ways to lower overall health care costs, then, is to control these chronic diseases. Drugs, in particular, have proven to be one of the most effective—and least costly—ways to do that.

A 2005 study published in *Medical Care* found that every additional dollar spent on medicines for diabetes, blood pressure, and cholesterol shaves $4 to $7 off other medical spending.[9]

A recent paper from the National Bureau of Economic Research found that Medicare ultimately saves $2.06 for every dollar it spends on medicines.[10] As Columbia Professor Frank Lichtenberg has pointed out, for every dollar spent on newer pharmaceuticals, we save $7.17 in hospital costs.[11]

In another study, the Agency for Health Care Policy and Research found that increased use of a blood-thinning drug would prevent 40,000 strokes annually, saving $600 million a year.[12]

It makes sense. A daily dose of Lipitor is a lot cheaper than emergency heart surgery.

SIPHONING MONEY AWAY FROM MEDICAL TREATMENTS

In just one year, Obamacare will siphon away enough money in taxes to launch two new medicines. The Tufts Center for the Study of Drug Development found that it takes $1.3 billion, on average, to research, develop, and bring a new drug to market.[13]

So with every passing year of Obamacare, the government will take out of industry coffers the very same dollars that otherwise could have helped create a new biologic like Rituxan, which revolutionized the fight against Non-Hodgkin's Lymphoma. Creating new drugs and treatments is expensive, and Obamacare's punitive taxes on the companies that create new drugs and medical devices could make it prohibitively so. By crippling research into future cures, more Americans will suffer, as our health care costs inflate. Who knows how many dollars—and lives—could be saved by a medical invention that obviates the need for, say, mammograms.

Put simply, new medicines and devices depend on investment. As biopharmaceutical firms and device manufacturers become less profitable, investors will flee for other sectors of the economy. Research and development money will dry up. The artificial lens of tomorrow might never be invented. And, in the end, countless patients will suffer more painful and shorter lives thanks to Obamacare.

CHAPTER 14

A LONG-TERM PONZI SCHEME

I f you've never heard of the CLASS Act, you're not alone. This provision within Obamacare might sound like a cleverly named education reform—or a bailout for unemployed Cary Grant wannabes. But it's much worse than that. In fact, it will dramatically transform the long-term care business in this country.

It will also be extremely costly. Future generations of taxpayers can look forward to shouldering billions upon billions in debt to pay for this new long-term care entitlement.

LONG-TERM CARE—A LONG-TERM PROBLEM

What is long-term care?

In a nutshell, it's the set of services that many elderly, chronically ill, or disabled people require to carry out basic activities of daily living—like getting dressed, bathing, cooking, or using the restroom.

When we think of long-term care, we often think of nursing homes, assisted-living facilities, or other institutions. But these services are increasingly being delivered at home by professional caregivers or family members, and the number of people who require them is growing. Today, nine million Americans over the age of sixty-five need long-term care; by 2020, that number will increase by a third.[1]

Medicare does not cover long-term care. So people who might need such care have two choices: They can purchase private long-term care insurance on their own or through their employer; or they can deplete their assets and rely on Medicaid, which covers *some* long-term services.

CLASS IS IN SESSION

Democratic health reformers chose to address the public's growing long-term care needs not by making it easier for Americans to secure private coverage, but by creating a massive new entitlement—the CLASS Program. Short for Community Living Assistance Services and Supports, CLASS thrusts the federal government into the long-term care business.

Here's how it works. Starting in 2011—or perhaps later, depending on how long it takes the Secretary of Health and Human Services to issue the relevant regulations—all workers whose employers decide to participate in the program will automatically be enrolled in CLASS. They'll have between $150 and $240 in premiums deducted from their paychecks each month—unless they formally opt out.[2]

Participants in the program will be eligible for cash benefits that range from $50 to $100 per day if they become disabled—that is, if they are unable to perform at least two activities of daily living. In order to qualify for the cash, participants must have paid premiums for at least five years prior to drawing benefits—and worked for three of those five years.

A FAILING BUDGETARY GRADE

Proponents of CLASS claim that the insurance scheme presents no risk to taxpayers because it will use workers' monthly premiums to pay out benefits. Better yet, they say, no less an authority than the Congressional Budget Office has estimated that CLASS will lower the federal deficit by $72 billion through 2019.[3]

Unfortunately, the CBO estimate of the program's first ten years is extremely misleading. The CLASS program will collect premiums for five full years before it has to remit its first cash benefit. (Remember, beneficiaries have to pay premiums for five years before they can get their hands on any cash.)

By counting ten years of premium collections—but only five years of payouts—the CBO can "calculate" that the program will post a net positive to the government's balance sheet.

In the years that follow, those purported savings will vanish.

By 2025, CLASS will disburse more than it takes in,[4] and in its third decade of operation, CBO estimates that the program "would add to budget deficits... by amounts on the order of tens of billions of dollars for each 10-year period."[5]

CBO is likely *underestimating* the potential for a CLASS-fueled fiscal train wreck.

ADVERSE SELECTION

The program is voluntary and open to all Americans, so it's likely that only people who think they'll need the benefits will sign up. If the insurance pool is comprised primarily of patients who will require costly payouts at some point, premiums will have to be higher to compensate. As premiums increase, comparatively healthier enrollees will drop their coverage. In insurance circles, this phenomenon is called "adverse selection."

In addition, CLASS will provide discounted coverage to students and low-income individuals—with initial premiums of just $5 a month.[6] Premiums for middle-income folks will have to shoot even higher to subsidize these low premiums.

"PONZI SCHEME OF THE FIRST ORDER"

Adverse selection in combination with artificially low premiums will cause a "death spiral," whereby steadily escalating premiums force out ever greater numbers of patients until there are not enough premium-paying customers to cover benefit payouts.

Indeed, Chief Actuary Richard Foster at the Centers for Medicare and Medicaid Services estimates that adverse selection problems will result in just two percent of potential participants signing up for the program.[7]

With a pool that small, it's a virtual certainty that participants will claim far more in benefits than they'll ever pay in premiums.

No wonder the Chief Actuary has said that CLASS is at "very serious risk" of being "unsustainable" and faces "a significant risk of failure."[8]

Democrat Senator Kent Conrad of North Dakota, the Chairman of the Senate Budget Committee, dubbed the CLASS Act a "Ponzi scheme of the first order."

Senate Finance Committee Chair, Democrat Max Baucus of Montana, once declared on the Senate floor, "Frankly, I am no fan of the CLASS Act myself."

Too bad both senators voted in favor of it.

CHAPTER 15

SELLING OUT SENIORS

According to the Congressional Budget Office, Obamacare will cost at least $938 billion over the next decade.[1]

So here's the big question: Who is going to pay for it?

The answer is... drum roll, please... senior citizens.

As it turns out, more than half of this bill will be covered through cuts in Medicare spending.

Medicare affects an enormous portion of the population. In 2008, it covered more than 45 million Americans. Roughly 38 million of them were sixty-five or older. The other 7 million were disabled.[2]

All told, the president's health care bill will cut Medicare by $575 billion over ten years, according to the Centers for

Medicare & Medicaid Services (CMS).[3] Seniors and the disabled are going to see their costs rise and their quality of care suffer.

Medicare is an expensive program, and it could certainly benefit from some streamlining. In fact, Medicare fraud has grown into a $60-billion-a-year business.[4]

But the legislation does virtually nothing to curtail fraud. Instead, it takes a slash-and-burn approach. Most troubling, the legislation attacks Medicare Advantage, the one aspect of Medicare that's working particularly well.

Under Medicare Advantage, private insurance companies offer an alternative to traditional Medicare. So it's not difficult to understand why the Democrats targeted this program. Big-government types detest Medicare Advantage because it outsources to the private sector. Obamacare will cut it by $202 billion over ten years, according to CMS.[5]

SLASHING MEDICARE ADVANTAGE

"If you like your health care plan, you'll be able to keep your health care plan, period," Obama declared while campaigning for his legislation. "No one will take it away, no matter what."[6]

That's certainly not true for the seniors on Medicare Advantage, who will see many of the benefits they've been enjoying vanish—along with their better health outcomes.

In 2011, the government will freeze payments to Medicare Advantage plans at current levels. Beginning in 2012, it will start actually reducing payments. Those cuts will then phase in over two to six years.[7]

The president claims that this is about "eliminating waste."[8] But the facts don't bear it out.

It's true that Medicare Advantage (MA) patients cost the government more than regular Medicare patients. But MA patients also get more—more benefits even than the government is paying for.

Medicare Advantage plans are HMO plans that are provided by private insurers. These plans offer far more choice than traditional government care, so they've become very popular in recent years.

The number of MA enrollees has doubled from 5.3 million in 2003 to 10.2 million in 2009.[9] Currently, about 22 percent of Medicare beneficiaries are in Medicare Advantage plans, and cuts to this program will affect a sizable proportion of our seniors—making them worse off.

Payments made from the government to Medicare Advantage HMOs have been, on average, about 10 percent higher than the cost of traditional, government-managed Medicare, the Congressional Budget Office found.[10] This is the "waste" to which President Obama was referring.

But wait. These HMOs offer patients extra benefits or premium rebates of 13 percent of traditional Medicare costs.[11] That means Medicare Advantage patients are getting 3 percent of additional benefits for free.

Some get vision and dental coverage—two things traditional Medicare doesn't cover. Some get better care for their chronic diseases. Others get a rebate on their premiums.

These additional benefits translate into better health for the patients who receive them. My colleague at the Pacific Research

Institute, John R. Graham, examined the data and discovered that Medicare Advantage patients did better than traditional Medicare patients on a whole range of outcomes.

Specifically, MA patients performed better on five key quality indicators, including breast-cancer screenings, diabetes testing, diabetes/lipid screening, annual flu vaccines, and prescribing beta blockers after heart attacks.

Notably, MA patients were screened and diagnosed earlier in cases of breast cancer, cervical cancer, colon cancer, and melanoma. Meanwhile, terminally ill MA patients had better access to hospice care.[12]

Many of those benefits are likely to disappear under Obamacare. Enrollment growth would consequently trail off. The Congressional Budget Office estimates "that enrollment in Medicare Advantage plans in 2019 would be 4.8 million lower" than it would be without Obamacare."[13]

That's a shame because Medicare Advantage is a real advantage. The Henry J. Kaiser Family Foundation found that MA fee-for-service plans gave patients benefits of $55.92 a month over and above what traditional Medicare offered in 2006. Other MA plans gave patients $71.22 a month in additional benefits.[14]

All those extras are likely to be dropped when Medicare Advantage faces its $202 billion cut. Or perhaps premiums will be increased for the patients in the program.

SHIFTING COSTS TO PRIVATE PAYERS

Medicare Advantage is also more cost-effective for taxpayers. Unlike its government-run brethren, Medicare Advantage doesn't shift costs onto the privately insured, which means that when MA is cut, and more people shift over to regular Medicare, those extra costs will be borne by the privately insured.

Let's use California as an example. In 2005, private insurers paid $129 of every $100 of hospital costs. That's because they had to subsidize Medicare patients—traditional Medicare paid only $74 for every $100 of hospital costs.

Medicare Advantage HMOs, on the other hand, covered almost all the costs they incurred—$99 out of every $100.[15]

When more patients are forced into traditional Medicare programs, the privately insured will have to pay more for their care. So by cutting Medicare Advantage, Obamacare isn't lowering costs at all—it's just shifting them to the privately insured.

THE ROAD TO RATIONING

Obamacare also creates an Independent Payment Advisory Board (IPAB), which will pave the way to rationing Medicare services.

All fifteen board members will be appointed by the president. The board itself is independent and unelected—so it's unaccountable for its decisions. None of the board members is required to represent the interests of seniors, the people actually affected by what policies the IPAB puts into place.

Starting in 2014, the board can advise Congress and the president on how to reduce per capita Medicare spending if it grows too fast. Its recommendations are not supposed to be used to raise taxes, change benefits, or ration care. Nevertheless, it's almost certain that IPAB proposals will lead to these outcomes indirectly.

For example, if IPAB's recommendations were used to cut payments to doctors and hospitals, Medicare patients would end up waiting longer to receive care—effectively rationing it.

In fact, Dr. Donald Berwick—the man President Obama has nominated to head CMS—has already spoken out in support of rationing.

In a 2009 interview, Dr. Berwick states, "The decision is not whether or not we will ration care—the decision is whether we will ration with our eyes open. And right now, we are doing it blindly."[16]

Dr. Berwick has also spoken highly of rationed care in the United Kingdom, extolling the virtues of the National Institute for Clinical Excellence (NICE), which is essentially a larger British version of IPAB. "I am romantic about the National Health Service," he once gushed. "I love it."[17] He has also noted that NICE has "developed very good and very disciplined, sci-entifically grounded, policy-connected models for the evalua-tion of medical treatments from which we ought to learn."

Apparently, Dr. Berwick thinks that Medicare should follow the United Kingdom's rationing model. So how has rationing worked for our neighbors across the Atlantic?

The Britain's Rarer Cancers Forum found that 20,000 patients died prematurely after being denied cancer medica-tion by NICE.[18] And that's just the tip of the iceberg, as we've already seen. NICE is anything but.

SHORT-CHANGING DOCTORS AND HOSPITALS

Finally, Obamacare will cut Medicare payments to hospitals that serve low-income patients by $22 billion. Payments for home care will be cut by $40 billion, and payments for inpatient and outpatient hospital services will be cut by $157 billion.[19]

Unfortunately, such measures will not eliminate much waste or fraud. Instead, they will exacerbate the terrible cost-shifting problems that already exist. As Medicare increasingly underpays, providers will need to cover their costs by raising prices on the privately insured.

Physicians are already underpaid by Medicare. A 2008 survey of doctors by The Physicians' Foundation found that 12 percent of doctors have closed their practices to Medicare patients.[20]

Richard S. Foster, the chief actuary for the Centers for Medicare and Medicaid Services, warns that Obamacare could exacerbate this problem.

"Providers for whom Medicare constitutes a substantive portion of their business could find it difficult to remain profitable and, absent legislative intervention, might end their participation in the program (possibly jeopardizing access to care for beneficiaries)."

Foster estimates that within a decade, about 15 percent of Medicare hospital-care providers will become unprofitable, making it difficult for seniors—especially those in rural areas—to get the care they need.

THE WRONG APPROACH

Today, over 12 percent of Americans are senior citizens—and that figure is growing rapidly as more and more baby boomers turn sixty-five. Assuming we live long enough, all of us will end up with Medicare coverage eventually.

Medicare is a big, expensive program—and costs do need to be contained. But Obamacare takes the wrong approach. It guts the best parts, exacerbates cost shifting, and sets the stage for future rationing.

This is hardly the right way to take care of our oldest citizens.

Perhaps this explains why seniors are so opposed to the bill. In June 2010—while the government was sending out $250 drug rebate checks to 10 percent of seniors—nearly 60 percent of older American's supported the repeal of Obamacare. Indeed, to counteract this rising sentiment, President Obama was forced to hold a televised town hall meeting with seniors to highlight the $250 checks and tout his health care bill.[21]

CHAPTER 16

REGULATING PROFITS

At a press conference in July 2009, President Obama said, "There have been reports just over the last couple of days of insurance companies making record profits, right now. At a time when everybody's getting hammered, they're making record profits, and premiums are going up."[1]

A few days later, House Speaker Nancy Pelosi ratcheted things up by accusing insurance companies of being "immoral." She went on to describe insurance companies as "the villains" in the health reform fight.[2]

As they pushed for Obamacare, the president and his allies routinely demonized insurance companies, often accusing them of making unfair profits.

It's certainly true that insurance premiums have been rising, but these increases are driven by costs—not profits.

In fact, insurance company profits have been anemic in recent years, and the industry as a whole is hardly a model of profitability. Accusing insurance companies of making "record profits" is like saying the Jamaican bobsled team had a stellar year because it didn't crash.

Every year, *Fortune* magazine issues a comprehensive analysis of America's largest corporations. In 2009, just forty-three of the industries examined turned a profit—and the health insurance sector ranked thirty-fifth. Indeed, it made just 2.2 cents in profit for every dollar in revenue. By contrast, the Internet services and retailing sector of the economy earned nearly 20 cents on every dollar.[3]

Plus, several of America's most well-known insurers—Kaiser Permanente, Blue Cross/Blue Shield of Michigan, and many others—operate as nonprofits.

Obamacare's proponents simply ignore such facts. They see only rising premiums—and so they wrongly assume that insurance companies earn too much money.

To remedy this "problem," Obamacare requires insurers to spend a designated percentage of their revenues on medical claims.

The presumption is that a high "minimum medical loss ratio," or MLR as this mandate is called, is an indicator of better care. If insurers only spend 15 percent on administrative expenses and trim their profits, the thinking goes, customers will get better value for their money.

Under the new law, plans in the "large group market" (i.e., most employer-provided insurance packages) will be required to spend 85 percent of premium dollars on clinical services beginning in 2011. Plans in individual and small-group markets will be required to spend 80 percent of premium dollars on clinical services.[4]

Despite the claims of Obamacare's proponents, though, high medical loss ratios will raise insurance prices, limit consumer choice, and make it difficult for insurers to offer many of the benefits that patients expect.

FALSE PREMISES

As we've seen, it's a myth that health insurance companies are turning huge profits; in fact, even the canny investor Warren Buffett has completely avoided *health* insurance companies, despite owning more than fifty domestic and foreign-based *other* insurance companies through his holding company, Berkshire Hathaway.[5] But Obamacare is based on this myth.

Obamacare also presumes that insurers spend too much on non-medical services, though there is no evidence to support this claim either. A report by the Centers for Medicare and Medicaid Services estimated that 86 percent of insurance premiums are already spent on medical care.[6] Similarly, according to regulatory filings, the six largest for-profit health insurers spent, on average, 85.1 percent of their premium dollars on medical care in 2009.[7]

What about administrative expenses? If insurers were forced to spend less money on bookkeeping and photocopying, wouldn't they be able to trim insurance premiums—and dedicate more money to medical care?

Not really. In fact, administrative costs can actually reduce waste and fraud and help keep premiums low. Cost-saving anti-fraud efforts and investments in health IT are considered administrative. As a study of California's insurance market by the Rand Corporation concluded, "Administrative costs and profits are not driving premium growth in California or nationwide."[8]

HIGHER PRICES, FEWER CHOICES

Prior to the passage of Obamacare, medical loss ratios had already been implemented in more than fifteen states. Such mandates resulted in higher premiums, less competition, and fewer choices, according to a 2006 study by Pricewaterhouse-Coopers, the world-renowned consulting firm.[9]

Consider New York and New Jersey, two states that enacted strict mandatory medical loss ratio requirements in 1993 for the individual and small group market.[10] Today, those states are home to some of the highest insurance prices in the country.

In New York, for example, the average annual premium in the individual market in 2009 was a whopping $6,630. In Missouri, the average annual premium was $2,725.[11] These prices are influenced, of course, by guaranteed issue, community rating, benefit mandates, and other regulations, as discussed elsewhere. But this comparison does help highlight the impact of minimum medical loss ratios.

How this mandate hurts competition is obvious. Minimum loss ratios favor large insurers who can afford to comply with them. Small firms might not be able to achieve the economies of scale that help big firms limit their administrative expenses. As small insurers are consolidated or driven out of the marketplace, only behemoths will remain, which means less competition and higher prices.

Minimum medical loss ratios can also hurt patient health by limiting choices and curtailing benefits.

Consider the many wellness initiatives that insurers have launched—disease management systems, discounts for those who regularly go to the gym, and the like. These programs help patients take better care of themselves by focusing on lifestyle changes. Such programs, though, are generally classified as administrative because customers don't have to see the doctor or visit the hospital to participate. The strict minimum loss ratio that Obamacare imposes will undoubtedly cut into the funding for these programs.

PERVERSE INCENTIVES

Ironically, Obamacare's minimum medical loss ratios could encourage insurance companies to raise premium prices—if they want to hold their profit margins (which, as we've seen, are not large)—or reclassify administrative expenses as medical expenses.

Indeed, shortly after Obamacare passed, WellPoint—one of the country's largest health insurers—reclassified more than half a billion dollars in expenses in order to help meet its target medical loss ratio.[12] These expenses mostly consisted of nurse hotlines and other wellness programs.[13]

Regulators are already considering "fixing" this unforeseen problem.[14] Doing so means legislators and bureaucrats will make arbitrary and ambiguous business and accounting decisions for insurers—and as the regulation mounts, it could easily drive some companies out of business, further reducing competition.

AN INITIATIVE THAT WON'T WORK

In July 2009, right around the time that President Obama lashed out against health insurance companies for "making record profits," the American Academy of Actuaries released a report on minimum loss ratios.

Its conclusion? "Minimum loss ratios do not help contain health care spending growth, ensure that health care services are appropriate and accurately billed, or address directly the quality and efficiency of health care services."[15]

Apparently, President Obama and his friends were too busy vilifying insurance companies to study the facts.

CHAPTER 17

UNDERMINING INSURANCE

O bamacare undermines the very concept of insurance.

The purpose of insurance is to protect you from a huge, unlikely, and unpredictable expense. You pay a small premium up front, and in return, the insurer agrees to pay for a massive cost that will probably never be incurred.

For example, you could purchase homeowner's insurance for, say, $100 per month, so that you'll be reimbursed $300,000 for damages in the improbable event of a flood or fire.

Similarly, you could buy auto insurance for $50 per month so that your $20,000 car would be replaced in the extremely unlikely event that it was stolen or destroyed.

That's how insurance works for most things.

But it's not how most health insurance works in the United States. And it's certainly not how health insurance will work under Obamacare, which will, in fact, make it difficult for any company to offer a health plan that functions like auto, home-owner's, or any other normal type of insurance.

PRE-PAYING FOR HEALTH CARE

As we've seen, Obamacare establishes new state-based exchanges where individuals and small businesses will be able to purchase health insurance. There will be four plan levels—Bronze, Silver, Gold, and Platinum.

Bronze plans will be expected to pay 60 percent of a patient's health care expenses; Silver plans, 70 percent; Gold plans, 80 percent; and Platinum plans, 90 percent.[1]

None of these plan types will simply cover catastrophic expenses. Instead, they are all designed to cover routine health care expenses. So owners of these plans will end up pre-paying their regular health expenses through a monthly premium.

Imagine if a grocery store offered such "insurance." You'd pay Safeway $1,000 per month. And in return you could purchase as much food as you could eat at an 80 percent discount.

Some might come out ahead with this plan. But actuaries would make it difficult to beat the system. They'd set the premiums high enough to ensure that the plan was profitable for Safeway. Thus, the vast majority of policy holders would pre-pay for more food than they needed, and, consequently, they'd lose money.

Of course, this wouldn't really be an insurance plan at all. It would be a pre-paid grocery plan—and not a very good one.

Or imagine if homeowner's insurance plans were designed this way. You'd pay a $2,000 monthly premium, and then you'd be reimbursed for 80 percent of all the money you spent on supplies like $2 light bulbs and $5 water filters. You'd spend a lot of money up front for the false sensation that you were getting your light bulbs for nearly free.

It just doesn't make sense.

But that's exactly how plans within the Obamacare exchange will work. Meanwhile, for plans outside the exchange, Obamacare will put intense pressure on them to function in a similar manner.

The new law will mandate "first-dollar" coverage for preventative care services. That will force insurance plans to cover almost every routine cost—including even the most minor events, like a doctor's checkup. Policy holders—and taxpayers—will simply end up pre-paying for their medical expenses.

In fact, Obamacare actually bans cost-sharing (what most people think of as a co-payment) for routine preventative care.[2] The law requires insurance providers to pay for the medical equivalent of light bulbs and dish soap.

ATTACKING HIGH-DEDUCTIBLE PLANS

Currently, many employer-sponsored insurance plans in the United States already function in this manner. They're very expensive and have low deductibles. Through their employers, people pay enormous premiums so that even the most trivial medical expenses are covered. It's one of the primary problems with American health care.

Unfortunately, most owners of these plans aren't aware of how much their insurance actually costs because their plans are subsidized by their employers. But people who don't have access to employer-subsidized care are very aware of how much insurance costs. Not surprisingly, they tend to prefer high-deductible policies. These plans are relatively inexpensive. They're designed to cover significant medical expenses that could disrupt your finances—like treating an injury, disease, or chronic condition.

In most states, it is still possible to buy this type of affordable health insurance, which covers only major costs. Such policies are called "high deductible" plans because their benefits don't kick in until after the policy holder has paid around a thousand dollars out-of-pocket.

High-deductible plans function like normal auto or homeowner's insurance—and they restore economic sanity to the health insurance market. They also hold the key to lowering health care costs in this country by putting consumers in control of their own spending, just as they are when they purchase groceries, computers, or virtually any other product or service.

Owners of high-deductible plans choose how they spend their health care dollars. Until their deductible is met, they pay out-of-pocket for most routine medical costs, including doctor's visits and prescription drugs—so they shop wisely and spend less money on superfluous items. Most important, they don't pre-pay—or overpay—for care they don't need.

Obamacare attacks high-deductible plans directly by banning cost-sharing for preventative services, which makes these plans more expensive. It also regulates some of these plans out of existence altogether. The new law caps deductibles at $2,000 for individuals and $4,000 for families. This is about one-third the level allowed under current law.[3]

Attacking high-deductible plans is terribly misguided.

The Blue Cross Blue Shield Association says their customers who are enrolled in high-deductible plans are almost 50 percent more likely to track health care expenses and search for information on physician quality than traditional health insurance plan enrollees. They are also 160 percent more likely to save money for future medical expenses.[4]

After analyzing multiple studies, the American Academy of Actuaries found that high-deductible, patient-centered plans reduce health care costs between 12 and 20 percent in the first year, and 3 to 5 percent in subsequent years.[5]

Additionally, these studies also found that high-deductible plan holders received the same amount of necessary care as individuals enrolled in traditional health insurance programs.

Critics of high-deductible plans often argue that policyholders forego routine, preventative care. But the studies don't bear this out. Participation in preventative programs actually increases under high-deductible plans.[6]

CAPPING HSA OPTIONS

One of the reasons high-deductible plans have been so effective to date is because of Health Savings Accounts (HSAs).

HSAs are special investment vehicles that are available to people with high-deductible plans. HSAs are similar to 401(k)s, but they're designed to help people save, not for retirement, but for medical expenses.

To qualify for an HSA, a person must own an insurance policy with a deductible of $1,200 or more, as of 2010. (For family policies, the deductible must be at least $2,400.)

Here's how HSAs work:

As of 2010, owners can deposit up to $3,050 (or $6,150 for families) per year into an HSA tax free. They can then spend that money, without incurring taxes, on most types of medical-related products and services.

The money they don't spend remains in the HSA and can be invested. Once an HSA holder turns sixty-five, the account can be used as a retirement fund, just like a 401(k). Money can be withdrawn for non-medical purposes without penalty. Such withdrawals are simply taxed as ordinary income.

In essence, HSAs allow those who don't have access to generous employer-sponsored plans to pay for medical care with pre-tax dollars. This levels the taxation playing field with those whose health care is already paid for, pre-tax, by an employer.

HSAs have been incredibly successful at helping people gain access to health care. Studies show that at least 30 percent of the 10 million Americans who have purchased HSA-eligible plans were previously uninsured.

Unfortunately, Obamacare lays the groundwork to vastly weaken the appeal of Health Savings Accounts. For starters, it places limits on the types of expenses for which HSA money can be used. (These new limits will also affect options similar to HSAs, including Flexible Spending Accounts, Health Reimbursement Accounts, and Archer Medical Savings Accounts.)

For example, under the new law, over-the-counter (OTC) medication will no longer be an acceptable medical expenditure by 2011.[7] So basic drugs like allergy or cold medicine won't qualify anymore as medical expenses that can be paid for through an HSA.

In some cases, this bizarre rule could actually penalize HSA holders for purchasing the less expensive version of the same drug. Ron Bachman, a senior fellow with the National Center for Policy Analysis, cites the following example:

"As a prescription drug, Claritin costs about $2.50 a day. The OTC price immediately dropped to $1 a day and it is now about 50 cents. By prescription, the heartburn drug Prilosec costs about $4 a day. It is now available OTC for as little as 50 cents a day. Obviously, it makes no sense to prohibit patients from making these kinds of lower-cost choices."[8]

THE DEVIL IS IN THE DETAILS

Other nitty-gritty regulations that could dramatically affect high-deductible plans are left to be worked out later by the secretary of Health and Human Services (HHS).

For example, under Obamacare, all insurance plans must now have a minimum actuarial value of 60 percent. "Actuarial value" is a rough measure of how generous a plan's benefits are. High-deductible insurance could be hit hard by this regulation depending upon whether HSA contributions can be included when calculating a plan's actuarial value. The law leaves this critical determination in the hands of the HHS secretary.[9]

The HHS secretary will also decide what preventative care insurance plans have to cover. The bigger that list of required covered services is, the more high-deductible plans might see dramatic price increases.

Already, HHS has established an Office of Consumer Information and Insurance Oversight (OCIIO) to help the federal government as it overhauls the insurance market. According to *Kaiser Health News*, the office will be focused on "writing rules to define when premium increases are 'unreasonable,' creating new coverage for people who can't get it because of health conditions and making sure insurers comply with consumer protections."[10]

President Obama promised on July 16, 2009, that "if you've got health insurance, you like your doctors, you like your plan, you can keep your doctor, you can keep your plan. Nobody is talking about taking that away from you."[11]

And yet, less than a year later, the president set the stage for reneging on that promise. In June 2010, the Departments of Labor, Treasury, and Health and Human Services issued regulations for existing health insurance plans that would supposedly "grandfather" them in under the terms of the old law, pre-Obamacare.[12]

Unfortunately, the rules are so restrictive that they would effectively outlaw many existing plans. Even the slightest changes—like increasing co-payments by more than $5 or increasing an employee's share of premiums by more than 5 percent—would revoke a plan's grandfathered status and force an individual or employer to comply with all of Obamacare's costly new mandates.[13]

For small businesses, the story's even worse. These firms would not be allowed to change insurers if they wanted to keep the same coverage for their employees—even if they could get a better deal elsewhere.[14] Obama's allies in organized labor, however, conveniently gained an exemption from this rule.[15]

As a result of these new regulations, administration officials acknowledge that at least 15 percent of American workers will lose their current coverage in 2011.[16] At worst, nearly 70 percent of workers—and 80 percent of those who work for small businesses—would find themselves forced onto different and probably pricier policies by 2013.[17]

Contrary to his promises, President Obama appears poised to "take away" the insurance policies of millions of Americans and shoehorn them into plans of his choosing.

CHAPTER 18

OBAMACARE'S BIGGEST LOSER

C hildren who attended the White House Easter Egg Roll in 2010 discovered that President Obama had made some big changes to the annual event.

The theme—Ready, Set, Go!—promoted health and wellness, and the official logo was a bunny wearing a headband and jogging shorts.[1] The grounds of the executive mansion were filled with exercise stations. And instead of candy, kids received goody bags containing fruit.

"One can only imagine the joy on young faces when they got their apple and their workout," quipped *Washington Post* columnist Michael Gerson.[2]

With the Easter Egg Roll coming just two weeks after the passage of the health care bill, the event was perfectly symbolic of

Obama's efforts to turn Americans—whether we like it or not—into a nation of health nuts.

On the surface, it seems logical for the government to encourage people to stay healthy. With medical costs spiraling upward and taxpayers on the hook for more and more of the country's health care expenses, maybe it's time for the government to step in and curb unhealthy behaviors before they develop into expensive health problems.

But the government's record on healthy living initiatives is dismal. Past government efforts have not only been unsuccessful, they've often worsened the very problems they set out to solve. And in the process, they've driven up overall health care costs. In many cases, we've become less healthy, and taxpayer dollars were wasted.

With Obamacare, history will almost surely repeat itself.

Fast food is unhealthy? Who knew?

Big Macs aren't healthy. Nor are Nacho Cheese Gorditas from Taco Bell.

This shouldn't surprise anyone—these days, fast food restaurants routinely advertise how unhealthy their food is.

Taco Bell patrons are surely aware that *gordita* is Spanish for "chubby."

When KFC unveiled its Double Down sandwich in 2010—which features two fried chicken patties, two pieces of bacon, and two slices of cheese and KFC's secret sauce—it advertised the sandwich with the slogan, "This product is so meaty, there's no room for a bun!"

Lawmakers in Washington, though, somehow became convinced that Americans only indulge in these delicacies because they are ill-informed. So when they wrote Obamacare, they inserted a provision requiring restaurants with twenty or more locations nationwide to display nutrition information next to most menu items.

Helping consumers make more informed decisions about what they eat seems like a laudable goal. However, there's no evidence that displaying calorie counts will make a dent in America's obesity epidemic.

Take food labeling. In 1994, the federal Nutrition Labeling and Education Act mandated that nutritional and caloric information be clearly displayed on all packaged foods. The idea was that if Americans knew the facts about what they were ingesting, they'd choose to eat healthier.

Yet since the program began, with calorie counts staring out at us from every bag of Fritos, Americans have become fatter. Between 1995 and 2007, the percentage of obese Americans increased by two thirds.

Menu labeling, too, has already been tried.

For years, most of the nation's large fast food chains have made nutritional information available on their websites. Many have also posted this information in brochures, on posters, and even on placemats at their restaurants.

In July 2008, New York City began requiring chain restaurants to provide calorie counts on their menus. Researchers from New York University and Yale studied the impact of this new regulation and published their results in *Health Affairs* in October 2009. Their findings were surprising. Researchers found that with the new mandate in place, calorie consumption in New York City actually *rose* 2.5 percent. Meanwhile, calorie consumption remained essentially unchanged in nearby Newark, New Jersey, which had no calorie mandates.[3]

Even though the number of New Yorkers who said they noticed calorie counts at fast food restaurants more than doubled, fewer than a quarter of those who noticed the calorie counts said it influenced their food decisions.[4] Surprisingly, "even those who indicated that the calorie information influenced their food choices did not actually purchase fewer calories."[5]

The New York City Department of Health did its own study on the menu mandate. The results were similarly unimpressive. According to the city's study, customers at only four of the thirteen fast food chains monitored for the study reported a reduction in caloric intake. Customers at one fast food chain reported consuming more calories after the law was enacted![6]

This shouldn't be surprising. People who pay attention to calories are not the same people whose habits need improvement. The problem isn't that Americans don't know that arugula is healthier than Nacho Cheese Gorditas; it's that many of us just don't care. Simply providing consumers with more nutritional information doesn't necessarily change behavior.

So who is most affected by the menu mandate? Restaurants, as they bear the enormous cost of compliance.

According to Dawn Sweeney, President and CEO of the National Restaurant Association, menu labeling regulations in the health care bill will "severely and negatively impact restaurants."[7]

Jim Skinner, the CEO of McDonalds, is more blunt. Even though McDonalds has voluntarily provided caloric information for over three decades, Skinner describes proponents of menu labeling as "professional naysayers" and "CAVE people." CAVE, according to Skinner, stands for "Citizens Against Virtually Everything."[8]

BREAKING NEWS: SMOKING IS UNHEALTHY

Under Obamacare, insurers are allowed to vary premiums based only on age, geographic area, the number of family members, and tobacco use.[9]

Alcoholic or drug addict? That's no big deal—you'll pay the same rates as a teetotaling triathlete, so long as you're the same age and live close to one another. If you occasionally light up a cigarette, though, you'll pay more for your insurance.

The bill also expands Medicaid to cover smoking cessation programs, though, again, it's doubtful what this will achieve (besides spending more tax dollars). Smokers already know that their habit is bad for them—they smoke because they choose to, not because they are ignorant. In fact, most smokers *overestimate* the risks. In the 1990s, one researcher found that the average smoker actually estimated his risk of developing lung cancer to be about 43 percent, even though that number is actually closer to 5 to 10 percent.[10]

OFFICE CALISTHENICS

The legislation also gives employers powerful incentives to ramp up workplace wellness programs.

Employees who can keep their weight, blood pressure, and cholesterol levels healthy will likely become eligible for steep discounts on their health insurance.

For the large group market, the law currently forbids discounts pegged to specific indicators of health from exceeding 20 percent of premiums. In 2014, thanks to Obamacare, employers will be allowed to offer discounts of up to 30 percent. In some cases, employers will be able to offer discounts of 50 percent to those employees who meet certain health-related standards.[11]

If you're not exercising every morning and eating a grilled chicken salad for lunch every day, this could cause your insurance premiums to skyrocket. According to two Harvard researchers, Kristin Voigt and Harald Schmidt, this provision "could cost individuals an extra $2,412 for not participating in workplace wellness programs—or an additional $6,688 for people with family coverage."[12]

In their study, Voigt and Schmidt worry that this provision will have a disproportionate impact on low paid workers who tend to be less healthy. They argue it will be a "threat to fairness and affordable care."[13]

Office calisthenics isn't too outlandish an idea. According to a survey by Hewitt Associates, a global consulting firm, "employers' appetite for penalizing workers for unhealthy behaviors is also on the rise."[14] The survey of more than 600 large employers representing 10 million employees "shows nearly one-half (47 percent) say they either already use or plan to use financial penalties over the next three to five years for employees who do not participate in certain health improvement programs."[15] This raises bigger and more troubling questions: just how coercive do we want government to be, and how much do we want it to push employers to coerce us?

A POUND OF CURE, OR A POUND OF FLESH?

The misguided enthusiasm for menu labeling, counseling to stop people from smoking, and other wellness programs is part of a broader enthusiasm among lawmakers for preventative medicine.

In 2007, while campaigning for president, then-Senator Barack Obama summed up his attitude toward the necessity of preventative medicine. "An ounce of prevention is worth a pound of cure. But today, we're nowhere close to that ounce."[16]

Obama was hardly alone in this view—it had long been the conventional wisdom among many on Capitol Hill. "Reform will mean higher-quality care by promoting preventative care so health problems can be addressed before they become crises. This, too, will save money," Democrat House Speaker Nancy Pelosi of California and Democrat Majority Leader Steny Hoyer of Maryland said in a 2009 *USA Today* opinion article.[17]

Unfortunately, Benjamin Franklin's folksy truism doesn't necessarily apply to the complex world of health care economics. In fact, the day before Pelosi and Hoyer took to the pages of *USA Today* to insist that preventative care will save money, the Congressional Budget Office came to the opposite conclusion.

"The evidence suggests that for most preventative services, expanded utilization leads to higher, not lower, medical spending overall," wrote CBO Director Doug Elmendorf.[18]

Richard Foster, the chief actuary of the Centers for Medicaid and Medicare Services, came to the same conclusion. "There is no consensus in the available literature or among experts that prevention and wellness efforts result in lower costs. Several prominent studies conclude that such provisions—while improving the quality of individuals' lives in important ways—generally increase costs overall," he explained in an official memorandum.[19]

The medical community has known this for years.

According to Alan Garber, the director of the Center for Health Policy at Stanford University, "The few studies that have compared preventative care to treatment have shown that either form of care can be cost-effective—or not—depending on how it's used. There's no magic to the idea of prevention, except that it sounds good."[20]

A 2008 report in the *New England Journal of Medicine* analyzed some 600 studies performed since 2000 that assessed the value of preventative care. Researchers concluded that although about 20 percent of preventative measures—including flu shots and colorectal cancer screenings—did save money, "the vast majority reviewed in the health economics literature do not."[21]

One obvious reason why prevention programs actually make health care more expensive is that healthier people live longer. Individuals who live into old age often require late-life care, which is enormously expensive. For example, it's incredibly expensive to care for someone with Alzheimer's.

As a study in the *British Medical Journal* concluded, "Elimination of fatal diseases by successful prevention increases health care spending because of the medical expenses during added life years."[22]

Indeed, those who like to eat and those who like to smoke actually *save* the government money.

Consider smoking. In 2001, Philip Morris conducted a study in the Czech Republic to determine whether smokers impose financial burdens on nonsmokers. The answer, not surprisingly, was that they do not. Since smokers don't live as long as nonsmokers, they don't burden society with expensive end-of-life care.[23]

In 2008, a peer-reviewed study in *PLoS Medicine* looked at medical costs attributable to smoking. The study found that spending on a nonsmoker who dies at age eighty-four is, on average, $100,000 more than on a smoker who dies—presumably aided and abetted by his bad habit—at a relatively youthful seventy-seven.[24]

The same is true for obesity. A few years ago, the Dutch Ministry of Health set out to discover whether or not obesity prevention is an effective means of lowering health care costs. The conclusion was blunt: "Obesity prevention is not a cure for increasing health expenditures."[25]

Of course, good health is to be treasured, and no one would suggest that smoking and obesity should be encouraged in order to cut health care costs. But government prevention programs don't work, don't cut health care costs, and worse, they are an infringement upon our most basic freedoms. What you eat and how you live are your own choices, and no government should ever make those decisions for you.

CHAPTER 19

YOUR HEMORRHAGING WALLET

The tax pledge that President Obama made as a candidate couldn't have been any clearer: "Under my plan, no family making less than $250,000 will see their taxes increase—not your income taxes, not your payroll taxes, not your capital gains taxes, not any of your taxes."[1]

He even went further than that. He promised that he would lower taxes for just about all of us. "I will cut taxes—cut taxes—for 95 percent of all working Americans."[2]

The president broke both these promises as soon as he signed Obamacare into law.

In one speech, Obama talked about the dangers of new taxes because health care costs are already out of control—and he promised to ease our tax burden. Yet his "reform" package goes in the opposite direction. It raises existing taxes and creates a slew of new ones.

Obamacare was supposed to make health care cheaper for all of us. Instead, it's going to drive up the price of everything from tax bills to wheelchairs.

When you add it all up, Obamacare will bring about the biggest tax increase in our country's history—$569 billion over the next decade.[3]

MEDICARE TAXES

First, there are the direct increases in federal taxes.

The Medicare payroll tax will rise dramatically for many taxpayers. Starting in 2013, individuals with incomes over $200,000 a year and families making more than $250,000 will see this payroll tax rise from 1.45 to 2.35 percent. That's a single tax increase of more than 60 percent.

Also in 2013, individuals and families earning more than $200,000 and $250,000, respectively, will face a new 3.8 percent Medicare tax on "unearned" income, such as interest, capital gains, annuities, royalties, rents, and dividends.

This new Medicare tax is estimated to enrich the government by $210 billion from 2013 to 2019. It's supposed to be a tax on the rich, but a lot of not-so-wealthy Americans will end up paying it as well, because many will eventually sell a home.

Under Obamacare, if the profit earned on any home sale exceeds the capital gains exemption of $250,000 for an indi-

vidual or $500,000 for a family, the excess amount will be sub-
ject to the new Medicare tax, in addition to capital gains taxes.

Unfortunately, this will amount to a new tax on retirement
savings because so many Americans rely on the long-term
appreciation of their homes to help fund their nest eggs.

CRUSHING SMALL BUSINESSES

Small businesses will also be disproportionately burdened
by Obamacare, as they'll end up paying many of the new taxes
that are supposed to hit only the wealthy. That's because small
business owners often classify their business income as personal income in order to avoid the more onerous corporate tax
system.

It's not hard for a small business owner's income to inch up
into that $200,000-and-above income tax bracket—even
though he or she is using most of the income as operating capital and taking home a much smaller amount.

Also, because many small business owners are both an
employer and an employee, they get dinged twice on some
taxes—like the payroll taxes that cover Social Security and
Medicare. One study found that 40 percent of the revenue
gained in an increase in the tax rate of the top two brackets
would be on business income.[4]

"I think the real impact is going to be on the mid-sized and
smaller companies, where profit margins are a lot more narrow, and in some cases are so narrow that the effect of the tax
will push a small minority of the companies from black to red,"

MassDevice.com's Brad Perriello says of Obamacare's new tax on medical device manufacturers.[5]

Small businesses are at the heart of the American economy—providing jobs for roughly half of all Americans working in the private sector.[6] They're going to be hard hit by Obamacare. Money that could have created jobs will instead go to Washington.

NO INDEX TO INFLATION

Even worse, none of these taxes is indexed to inflation.

So as incomes rise—as they invariably do over time—more and more people will be subjected to these so-called taxes on the wealthy.

Twenty years from now, a person earning $200,000 would be the equivalent of a person earning $92,000 today, assuming 4 percent inflation.[7] Within thirty years, the tax would hit people earning today's equivalent of $62,000. And in fifty years, this "high-roller" tax would kick in at today's equivalent of $29,000.

These taxes will be waiting for you, your children, and your grandchildren.

BUT, WAIT, THERE'S MORE

A number of other taxes will also pummel Americans in 2013. And proponents of Obamacare can't even pretend that these taxes are targeted at the wealthy, as those who can least afford to pay will be hit hardest.

Obamacare halves the amount of money—from $5,000 to $2,500—that people can set aside in Flexible Spending Accounts (FSAs) to pay for medical expenses.

FSAs enable about 16 million Americans[8] to use pre-tax dollars to purchase ordinary medical services and supplies—like eyeglasses, dental work, over-the-counter medicines, prescription co-pays, and insurance deductibles. The sickest members of society, those with chronic illnesses, have extraordinary medical expenses, so they tend to rely more heavily on these accounts.

FSAs are designed to lower costs for routine medical expenses, and millions of American families save money with them. If your child needs braces, for example, you can pay for them tax-free by setting aside extra money in an FSA.

But Obamacare has gutted the program. Not only has the expense threshold been cut in half, but starting in 2011, FSAs can no longer be used to pay for over-the-counter medications—even drugs like Claritin or Prevacid—unless specifically requested by a doctor.

TAXING THE SICK AND INJURED

Obamacare also reduces the annual tax deduction for medical expenses. Right now, a person can deduct medical expenses that exceed 7.5 percent of his or her adjusted gross income. But starting in 2013, if you're under sixty-five, you can deduct medical expenses only if they exceed 10 percent of your income.

This change harms the middle- and lower-class people the president claims he wants to help—and falls disproportionately on the unhealthy: half of those who currently take advantage of this deduction make less than $50,000 a year. And the people who benefit most from this deduction are the sick and injured.

CADILLAC PLANS AND BRACKET CREEP

Other taxes will be phased in later.

People whose employers offer them top-of-the-line health insurance will be penalized for the privilege.

In 2018, so-called gold-plated Cadillac plans will be subject to a whopping 40 percent excise tax. The tax will ensnare employer-sponsored policies with premiums higher than $10,200 for individuals and $27,500 for families. This hefty new tax is expected to bring the government $32 billion in just the first two years.[9]

This tax, like so many other Obamacare taxes, won't be adjusted for inflation. It might take ten, twenty, or even thirty years, but sooner or later, every employer-sponsored policy will be subject to this 40 percent tax.

That's exactly what happened with the Alternative Minimum Tax (AMT), which was implemented four decades ago to prevent the ultra-wealthy from avoiding taxes altogether. The AMT originally targeted just 155 super-rich Americans who were paying no taxes. By 2009, about 4 million Americans were paying the AMT, and in some cases individuals earning under $50,000 could end up paying this oppressive tax.[10]

"Bracket creep" is when inflation drives you into a high tax bracket. Obamacare's bracket creep means taxpayers will be funneling a whole lot more money to the government in the years ahead.

Making matters worse, the cost of health insurance tends to rise faster than income. The Kaiser Family Foundation found that from 1999 to 2009, overall inflation was 28 percent. Earnings rose 38 percent. But health insurance premiums rose a whopping 131 percent.[11] If premiums continue rising at this pace, it will take only a few years before the average plan is deemed a Cadillac plan under the law.

MEDICAL TAXES

Obamacare doesn't just tax individuals. It also taxes businesses, and those costs will ultimately be passed back to consumers in the form of higher prices.

As we've seen, the government is hitting pharmaceutical firms with steadily increasing tax fees: $2.5 billion in 2011; $3 billion a year from 2012 to 2016; $4.2 billion in 2018; and $2.8 billion in 2019 and beyond. Not only will those fees dampen the development of new medicine, they'll also hit patients in the form of higher prices for drugs and medicine.

Meanwhile, starting in 2011, medical device companies will pay a 2.3 percent excise tax on most devices they sell, excluding eyeglasses, contact lenses, and hearing aids. This tax is expected to extract some $20 billion from the industry.

As a result, doctors and hospitals will pay more for CT scanners, intravenous bags, wheelchairs, and the like. Patients will pay more for heart stents, pacemakers, and other life-saving inventions.

DRIVING UP INSURANCE PRICES

Insurers will pay even more. They have to fork over to the government $8 billion a year starting in 2014 and $14.3 billion annually four years after that. The insurance levy will then increase every year at the rate of premium growth.

Obama promised to get tough with the insurance industry, but taxes like these will only make life tough for American families.

PricewaterhouseCoopers (PWC) found that these new taxes will increase the average cost of a family insurance plan by almost $476 a year.[12] And PWC's estimate was based on an earlier version of Obamacare, in which the taxes faced by these industries were actually lower than in the final bill.

In fact, PWC estimated that, under Obamacare, the average family would pay $20,700 more for insurance between 2010 and 2019 than that family would have paid in the absence of reform.[13]

That's not the only study that found that Obamacare will raise the cost of insurance. WellPoint, the country's largest insurer, looked at data from fourteen states. It found premiums would increase for the average consumer in every one of those states. (The study was conducted using an earlier version of Obamacare that was very similar to the final version.)

Who will be hit hardest by government-inflated insurance prices? Young people and small businesses.

In 2009, the average monthly premium for a 25-year-old man in Richmond, Virginia, was $66. WellPoint found that under Obamacare, that premium would skyrocket to $168. That's a 155 percent increase![14]

The average 25-year-old male in Louisville, Kentucky, has it even worse. Coverage costs him $61 a month. The reform would triple his premium to $181.[15]

WE HAVE A SITUATION

With more than 2,400 pages of regulations, Obamacare doesn't know when to quit. There's a tax for just about everything. Even tanning salons.

Seriously.

As mentioned in chapter 4, a new 10 percent tax on indoor tanning will go into effect as of July 2010. Anyone who's ever watched an episode of *Jersey Shore* knows that this will burn a certain segment of the population. Why were tanning salons singled out over, say, ice cream shops? Nobody knows. Perhaps Senator Harry Reid has a personal vendetta against JWoww or Pauly D.

Many tanning salons are small businesses owned by women. A 10 percent increase in the price of their services could easily force them to fire employees or shut down altogether. The tax is a $2.7 billion fist-pump for the government over the next decade, but it's a punch in the face of folks like Snooki.

The Jersey Shore lifestyle—gym, tan, and laundry—just got a whole lot pricier.

So did everything else under ultraviolet light.

CHAPTER 20

A CANCEROUS DEFICIT

O n Thursday, March 18, 2010, the Congressional Budget Office (CBO) released a last-minute score of the Obamacare bill. The CBO estimated that it would trim the deficit by $138 billion over the following ten years.

That CBO score changed history.

At the time, nearly fifty House Democrats remained undecided on the bill. But with the CBO's prediction of a deficit reduction, wavering Democrats now had all the cover they needed.

Democrat Congresswoman Betsy Markey of Colorado immediately announced she'd vote "yes."

So did Democrat Mark Schauer of Michigan and Democrat Bart Gordon of Tennessee (who had previously stated that he would not vote for any bill that added "one nickel to the national deficit").

A number of other Democrats quickly followed.

Three days later, on March 21, the House voted 219 to 212 to approve the Senate's version of Obamacare.[1]

President Obama himself declared that the legislation was "one of the biggest deficit reduction measures in history."[2]

But was it really? The facts suggest just the opposite.

FRONT-LOADING TAXES

Less than two months after President Obama signed the health care bill, the CBO released a new estimate of the cost— attributing an additional $115 billion in discretionary spending and implementation expenses, which hadn't been included in the original tally. That brought the total cost of Obamacare to over $1 trillion from 2010 to 2019.[3] It also wiped out most of the $138 billion of deficit reduction that proponents had originally claimed.

In fact, upon close examination, every penny of Obamacare's supposed "savings" is an illusion—achieved through a series of legislative and accounting gimmicks.

For starters, the law imposes huge new taxes in 2011, but the major benefits don't kick in until 2014. So the bulk of the spending doesn't start until nearly halfway through the CBO's measurement period.

As a result, over the first ten years, from 2010 to 2019, Obamacare's high costs are negated by several years of benefit-free taxation. Once benefits kick in, the program will hemorrhage money.

A more honest assessment of Obamacare's full cost would look at the decade starting in 2014, when most benefits start. Republican Senator Judd Gregg of New Hampshire did exactly that.

"They don't start the spending programs until the year 2014," explained Gregg. "When all this new spending occurs, this bill will cost $2.5 trillion over that ten-year period."[4]

Indeed, the Senate Budget Committee, of which Senator Gregg is the ranking member, found Obamacare will cost $2.5 trillion over ten years.[5] "The bill is front-loaded with tax hikes and spending cuts in the first few years with most of the new spending starting after 2014, effectively 'hiding' the true huge growth in government," the committee found.

Some put the cost even higher. According to Michael Cannon, director of health policy studies at the Cato Institute, "the actual cost of the bill is nearly $3 trillion." In addition to pointing out several other budgetary gimmicks, Cannon notes that the bill contains $1.5 trillion in hidden taxes created by the individual mandate.[6]

"UNSUSTAINABLE ON A PERMANENT BASIS"

The chief actuary of CMS, Richard S. Foster, also found that Obamacare would not reduce the deficit—even over the first decade.

"Overall national health expenditures under the health reform act would increase by a total of $311 billion."

Foster found that the new revenue collected in the bill "would be more than offset through 2019 by the higher health expenditures resulting from the coverage expansions."[7]

Foster also noted that several cost-cutting measures contained in the bill probably won't survive, which would drive up costs even higher. "Reductions in payment updates to health care providers, based on economy-wide productivity gains, are unlikely to be sustainable on a permanent annual basis."

Indeed, less than three months after the legislation was passed, Congressional Budget Director Doug Elmendorf gave a presentation on health costs and the deficit at the Institute of Medicine. "Rising health costs will put tremendous pressure on the federal budget during the next few decades and beyond," stated one of the slides. "In CBO's judgment, the health legislation enacted earlier this year does not substantially diminish that pressure."[8]

Moreover, noted economist Douglas Holtz-Eakin, who headed up the Congressional Budget Office from 2003 to 2005, estimates that Obamacare will increase the budget deficit by $554 billion in its first ten years, and will add another $1.4 trillion to the deficit in its second ten years.[9]

THE DOCTOR FIX

In addition to skewing the numbers by front-loading taxes, proponents of Obamacare used other tricks to hide the program's true costs.

An early draft of the health care legislation, for example, included what's known as the "doctor fix." This bit of legislation would have given $208 billion over ten years to physicians who participate in Medicare. The "fix" is likely what turned the American Medical Association into a supporter of reform.[10]

Because Democrats were confident they could pass this provision as a stand-alone bill, they simply stripped the "doc fix" from the Obamacare draft and created a separate piece of legislation. That's how you make a bill that will cost billions look like it will save billions—take out one of the most expensive provisions and put it into a different bill. At the time this book went to press, temporary doc fix bills had already been approved by the House and the Senate. If the original doc fix had been included in Obamacare, the CBO says it would have increased the deficit by $59 billion in the first ten years.[11] Indeed, it was only by removing the fix that Democrats were able to claim the bill would reduce the deficit.[12]

A HISTORY OF UNDERESTIMATING

It's no surprise that Obamacare will cost us more than the president claims. Government has a long history of underestimating the costs of its programs.

Exhibit A: Medicare. In 1965, when Medicare was enacted, the House Ways and Means Committee predicted that spending for Part A, the hospital insurance program, would cost about $9 billion in 1990. What did we actually spend that year on Part A? $67 billion. That's more than seven times as much as estimated.

In 1967, the committee estimated that the entire Medicare program would cost $12 billion in 1990. It ended up costing $110 billion.[13]

So if Obamacare ends up costing ten times more than expected... don't be too surprised.

GOING FROM BAD TO WORSE

Obamacare could not have come at a worse time.

In 2008, the annual federal budget deficit was a record high $459 billion—nearly three times larger than the previous year's deficit. Clearly, the government was spending way beyond its means.

By 2009, our nation's political leaders were completely out of control, spending taxpayer dollars with reckless abandon. The federal government spent $3.5 trillion even though its revenues were only $2.1 trillion, taking the annual budget deficit soaring to $1.4 trillion—almost nine times higher than it had been just two years earlier.[14]

It was an historic shift in government behavior.

Past increases in spending had been in proportion, more or less, to America's Gross Domestic Product (GDP). From 1950 until 2008, federal spending hovered at around 20 percent of GDP. But in 2009, it jumped to 25 percent.[15] For the first time since the Second World War, the federal government had seized a significantly larger portion of the nation's economy.

The annual deficits, of course, pile on to the debt. America's Gross Federal Debt was $11.9 trillion in 2009. That's roughly six times what the federal government earned that year.

Deficit spending with a debt that high just isn't sustainable in the long term. It's like having $300,000 of credit card debt, yet continuing to spend $80,000 a year while earning a $50,000-a-year salary.

Before Obamacare was even passed, America's debt was already projected to skyrocket to $15.1 trillion in 2011.[16] Now the situation is far worse.

Nobody knows exactly how much it will cost over the long term. But one thing is certain: the final price tag is more than we can afford.

CHAPTER 21

THE DOCTOR IS OUT— PERMANENTLY

During a speech to the American Medical Association in June 2009, President Obama touched on one of the biggest crises facing America's health care system—a shortage of primary care doctors. Obama declared that health reform should "do more to reward medical students who choose a career as a primary care physician."[1]

Unfortunately, Obamacare threatens to exacerbate our nation's shortage of primary care doctors. In fact, just months after the passage of Obamacare, many doctors throughout the country chose to close up shop.

What's worse, since the new law extends health insurance to 34 million Americans who previously lacked coverage, the

president's reform plan is sure to make the doctor shortage
more acute in the years to come.

PRIMARY CARE DOCS ARE GOING THE WAY OF THE DODO

Primary care physicians are on their way to becoming an
endangered species in the medical profession. Half a century
ago, one in two doctors practiced general medicine. Today,
only three in ten doctors are in the field.

And the gap is growing. Since 1997, the number of medical
students specializing in primary care has dropped by more
than half.[2]

The current doctor shortage shouldn't come as a surprise to
anyone who has tried to schedule a physical in recent years. In
New York City, for instance, patients have to wait an average of
twenty-four days for a basic physical, according to a 2009 study
by the consulting firm Merritt Hawkins. In Los Angeles, the wait
is fifty-nine days, and in Boston, a whopping sixty-four days.[3]

Demographics dictate that the shortage is certain to worsen.
As more and more Baby Boomers reach old age over the next
decade, the demand for primary care will increase dramatically, given that older Americans require greater levels of medical attention.

Recognizing this trend, the American Academy of Family
Physicians warned in 2009 that the United States would be
short 40,000 family doctors in just ten years' time.[4] Today, medical schools produce one primary care doctor for every two
who are needed.

But it's not just primary care doctors that are in short supply. According to the Association of American Medical Col-
leges, the overall doctor shortage could reach 124,000 by 2025.[5]

The dearth of doctors could take root even sooner. A 2009
Merritt Hawkins survey of primary care physicians revealed
that 10 percent of respondents were planning to leave medicine within three years.[6]

These numbers are scary by themselves. But here's the
kicker: none of them takes into account the fact that Obamacare will almost certainly exacerbate the doctor shortage.

THE COMING PHYSICIAN EXODUS

A poll of physicians conducted in 2009 by *Investor's Business
Daily* found that 45 percent of doctors would consider early
retirement if Obamacare passed.[7]

Even more unsettling, Obamacare may well dissuade
would-be physicians from ever donning a stethoscope. The
same *Investor's Business Daily* study found that two-thirds of
practicing physicians believed that fewer students would apply
to medical school if Obama's health care plan passed.

Many doctors have taken the enactment of Obamacare as
their cue to exit the medical profession. For instance, Dr. Ger-
alyn Ponzio, a primary care physician in New Jersey, closed her
practice shortly after the law's passage. When asked if Obamacare drove her to quit the business, she explained that it
"was a very big part of it." [8]

Dr. Joseph M. Scherzer, a dermatologist from Scottsdale,
Arizona, tells a similar story. After health care reform passed,

Dr. Scherzer posted a sign on the door of his practice with the following message: "If you voted for Obamacare, be aware these doors will close before it goes into effect."[9]

According to Dr. Scherzer, "Most physicians I've heard from feel the same way."

With Obamacare micromanaging how doctors practice medicine, it's no wonder so many physicians are leaving the business. For example, under the new law, if doctors serving Medicaid patients fail to adhere to the arbitrary treatment guidelines set by the secretary of Health and Human Services, they'll have to take a severe pay cut—even if the doctors believe their patients would be better served with alternative courses of treatment.[10]

"If you don't go by these guidelines," said Dr. Richard Armstrong, a surgeon and member of Docs 4 Patient Care, "you won't be able to bill Medicare or the insurance companies that participate in the exchanges."[11]

INCREASING DEMAND

Obamacare won't just reduce the number of practicing physicians in the United States. Almost by definition, the law will drastically increase demand for doctors in all specialties. After all, the package is projected to extend insurance (by 2019) to 34 million Americans who are currently uninsured. With more people covered by health insurance, more people will be demanding medical services.

Residents of Massachusetts have experienced this phenomenon firsthand. Since the Bay State enacted Obama-style health reforms in 2006, 440,000 people have been added to the insurance rolls, including Medicaid or government-funded plans.[12]

Despite their brand new insurance policies, many struggle to find a doctor. Droves of doctors have quit, retired, or moved out of state. A family care doctor in Amherst told NPR in 2008 that eighteen of her colleagues left in the wake of Massachusetts' reform.[13] One clinic in Western Massachusetts has a waiting list of 1,600 patients.[14]

Obamacare will expand the Bay State system nationwide, with dire consequences. If America's supply of physicians goes down and demand increases, one of two things must happen. Either the price of health care will increase, or government bureaucrats will control prices and ration care.

A combination of these two outcomes has taken root in Massachusetts. Not only have health costs in the Bay State risen faster than the national average, but state officials have considered implementing a system of capitation, whereby health care providers are paid a fixed amount per patient.

MORE PATIENTS, FEWER DOCTORS

With Obamacare, our future is one of fewer doctors, more patients, and longer waits. Maybe Congress should buy magazine subscriptions for all those doctors' waiting rooms that will soon be as packed as the Superdome after Hurricane Katrina.

CHAPTER 22

OBAMACARE IN 2050

April 15, 2050
The Honorable Tiffany Rodham-Clinton
United States Senator (Democrat, New York)
Washington, D.C. 20510

D ear Senator Rodham-Clinton:
First of all, congratulations on your new position. It really is remarkable that the Empire State is represented in Washington by the granddaughter of former Senator Hillary Clinton. Your November defeat of Governor Jack W. Bush reminded me of the decades-long rivalry between your families. I read about this in my high school American history class. Your Senate race brought the twentieth century to life for me.

Anyway, I am writing to alert you to my experiences in the Federal Health System. As my senator, I hope you will do what you can to improve the quality of the medical attention that average patients, like me, are seeing.

About six months ago, I was racing around Central Park in my jet pack. I have a light and agile model I like to use for recreation on weekends. This is not one of those squishy-suspension models that commuters use.

As I was going around a bend, however, it petered out. I fell from a height of about fifty feet. Luckily, I hit a tree branch, which slowed my fall and probably saved my life. The bad news is that I hit the asphalt and hurt my ankle. Also, the jet pack was very hot, and part of its tail pipe burned my lower back as I fell.

I lay flat on the ground—dazed, confused, and in serious pain. A few joggers neutralized their reduced-gravity shoes long enough to pull me to the side of the road. I used my Tele-PathIc forehead chip to summon an ambulance.

And that's when the real pain started.

I had heard that people had to wait a long time for ambulances. Only when I needed one did I realize how bad the problem is.

New York City used to pride itself on the speedy response time of its ambulances. Unfortunately, about forty years ago, all of that began to unravel.

As I remember from my American history textbook, after Congress passed health reform, and President Obama signed it (before becoming overwhelmed by that awful mess with the Iranian nuclear bomb and the BP oil spill in the Gulf of Mexico), New York was just one of many cities that began to drown in their Medicaid budgets.

When the federal government forced states and cities to increase their Medicaid populations under Obamacare,

Gotham had to cut back somewhere. So, the city chopped ambulances and paramedics assigned to the Fire Department. Of course, the budget cutbacks also cost many firefighters their jobs. Some firehouses even closed. The result was more fires with fewer engines to battle them. The greater number of fire victims had to wait longer for the smaller number of ambulances to attend to them.

Thinking about that, I sort of felt lucky while I sat on the asphalt for three hours waiting for an ambulance to show up. At least I was not dying of smoke inhalation, like those poor concertgoers who gasped for air for an entire afternoon awaiting ambulances on the day Britney Spears Hall burned to the ground. But I was also amazed to think that, despite my Tele-PathIc forehead chip, I would have received faster ambulance service forty years ago.

An ambulance finally came by and took me to the Chuck Schumer Memorial Hospital. I saw the huge lines of people waiting to get inside for treatment. "Lucky me," I thought. "I'm in an ambulance. They'll see me right away."

Wrong.

I was wheeled out of the ambulance and placed on a gurney with that famous 5-D "CSM" hologram that was the pride of Manhattan's finest hospital. I had the privilege of staring at it overnight while I waited to see a doctor. I wondered, what on earth could be wrong?

That's when I remembered something else from my history book.

Soon after Obamacare passed, doctors retired by the thousands. Most of them did not like idea of the secretary of Health and Human Services making decisions about whom to treat, how quickly, and with which drugs and medical devices.

Even worse, as Congress kept playing games with reimbursement formulae, doctors saw their Medicare- and Medicaid-related incomes fall. As taxes rose on their income bracket, these doctors felt squeezed, as in one of those waffle irons that they used to make, until the Kitchen Accident Prevention Authority decided they were too dangerous and banned them outright.

Doctors abandoned the profession in bigger numbers, and medical school enrollment kept falling. Pretty soon, the only doctors were those from Third World countries like Chavezuela and Cuba. (By the way, didn't Fidel Castro look great on *60 Minutes* on MSNBCBS the other night? Alive and well at age 124!)

Dr. Rafael Gomez, an internist from Havana, finally saw me eighteen hours after I arrived. He did some basic examination with his hands and said he wanted to check out my ankle with a device called an MRI. I had heard about these machines. Unfortunately, he explained, it was broken... again. It seems that few such devices were invented after about 2020.

My grandma told me something about a medical-device tax that cut into these companies' incomes. Apparently, Obamacare's taxes on capital gains and dividends chopped into the investment capital that these companies needed to grow and survive. So, they didn't.

Dr. Gomez asked me if I could come back in a while. Perhaps the MRI would be fixed, if the spare parts came in. Otherwise, some random, unemployed engineer in the waiting room might be able to cobble something together. (There are so many of them walking around with nothing to do these days, as you know, Senator. As my economics professor whispered to me at school the other day, fearing he could be fired for saying such a thing, the 65 percent top income tax rate and the 25 percent VAT needed to pay for Obamacare really do slow the economy.)

I asked Dr. Gomez if he might have some strong anti-inflammatories to deaden the pain and swelling until I could return for a follow-up visit in about two months. He urged me not to raise my hopes about seeing him again so soon. Without an ambulance, he said, who knows when I might come back?

As for the anti-inflammatories, he said that something called the Department of Patient-Centered Cost Research, Application, and Policy (PCCRAP) decided years ago that such drugs only could be used for broken bones; and until he could use the MRI to prove my ankle was broken, he couldn't give me any pills—or he might lose his license. Still, he told me he liked me and would try to get me bumped up in the queue.

I will never forget Dr. Gomez's final words to me: "Take two aspirin and call me in the morning."

I found a crutch standing in the corner of an empty examination room. No one seemed to notice that I used it to hobble home.

So, Senator, here I am. My ankle is killing me. The burn on my back could use something other than ice, I suppose.

(Schumer Memorial's dermatologist passed away last year and has yet to be replaced.) I am not sure how to fix all of this. But as Earth's fourth wealthiest country—after China, India, and Texas—I have to wonder: Is this the best we can do?

Best wishes,
Derek Jeter IV

CHAPTER 23

IDEAS FOR REFORM

To turn a phrase, there ought *not* to be a law; Obamacare should be booted from the U.S. Code and onto the ash heap of history.

Think it can't be done? Guess again—Congress has reversed course on health care reform before.

On July 1, 1988, Congress passed the Medicare Catastrophic Coverage Act and raised premiums on seniors to finance this new benefit.[1] Retirees went ballistic, and in one of the most memorable pieces of news footage ever, an angry mob of elderly Americans confronted then-House Ways and Means Committee chairman Dan Rostenkowski, a Democrat from Illinois. They literally surrounded his car, smacked his hood with picket signs, and chased him down the street on foot.[2]

As the late Republican Senator Everett Dirksen of Illinois once said: "When I feel the heat, I see the light."[3] On November 23, 1989, Congress voted to repeal this wildly unpopular legislation.[4]

IT'S NOT TOO LATE FOR REPEAL

The same thing could happen to Obamacare. Public-opinion surveys consistently show that Obamacare's unpopularity only grows as Americans learn more about it. A May 22 to 23, 2010, Rasmussen survey of 1,000 likely voters showed that 63 percent want Obamacare repealed.[5] If voters make that displeasure known in congressional elections, voting against supporters of Obamacare and voting for those in favor of repealing it, things could change dramatically.

Republicans are carrying the anti-Obamacare banner. To overturn the law they would need to secure 288 House votes and 67 in the Senate to withstand Obama's veto of any repeal measure. That's a tall order. But ground gained in 2010 could make 2012, when Obama faces re-election, a different story. A change in the White House and further changes in Congress could make repeal not just possible, but even likely, if we the people are insistent enough about it.

REAL REFORM

If the court challenges to Obamacare fail, and it's up to a new Congress and a new president to shred the old law and come up with a new one, here's what they should do: craft real reform that covers the uninsured without destroying individual freedom, quality treatment, medical innovation, and the economy.

A true, patient-centered health care reform bill would follow these ten principles:

1) Promote private ownership within a thriving individual health insurance marketplace.

Real reform requires a brand-new model for health coverage. Employers do not provide their workers with auto insurance, home insurance, life insurance, or fire insurance, and they shouldn't be expected to provide health insurance either. As we've seen, this anomaly comes from the wage controls that were imposed by the government during World War II, when companies decided to compensate employees with health insurance since they couldn't give them raises. The war has been over since 1945. So America is seven decades late in changing this arbitrary, outdated system.

Americans should be free to purchase individual health care plans. This would be their private property—just like their savings accounts, retirement portfolios, and life-insurance policies.

If companies or other private organizations want to provide group health insurance, that's fine; there could even be something like Rotary Health for Rotarians and Yankee Health open to Yankees fans across America. Freedom and competition should be the rule. Health insurance companies should compete for our business.

The goal of proper health care reform is to allow maximum choice within a flexible and innovative market guided by entrepreneurs and creative companies. What we have under

Obamacare is a system designed by power-seeking politicians, mandate-wielding bureaucrats, and big business and labor union lobbyists.

2) Make health coverage portable.

If American workers—rather than their bosses—manage their own health plans, they can carry them from job to job, city to city, or even when they go back to school or take time off for personal or family reasons.

Such portability would end "job lock"—staying trapped in a bad job because you don't want to lose your health insurance. Employers are likelier to treat their employees better if they can't use coverage as a shackle.

3) Allow individuals and families to buy health insurance with tax-free dollars.

How can Americans pay for such individual insurance?

Congress should change the federal tax code so that individuals and families can deduct health care premiums from their taxes.

Companies, but not their workers, can write off the cost of coverage. Correcting this unfair imbalance would immediately put privately owned insurance within the reach of most of the 176 million Americans currently enrolled in company-owned health plans.[6] Companies could then compete to offer tax-free, supplemental compensation to allow employees to buy additional insurance (useful for employees with preexisting conditions), if they wish. The more companies got out of the business of being the primary health care insurance provider, the more they could hire employees who produce value rather than employees whose job it is to shuffle administrative paper and keep up with the government's latest reams of regulations.

4) Universalize Health Savings Accounts.

Congress should allow universal access to Health Savings Accounts (HSAs), where individuals can keep tax free dollars to pay for standard medical expenses. HSAs are coupled with lower-cost, high-deductible catastrophic plans. Car insurance pays for fixing collision damage, while drivers themselves reach into their pockets for oil changes. Similarly, catastrophic insurance buys treatment after a heart attack, for example, while patients will use their HSA funds for things like new eyeglasses.

When millions more Americans are using their own, tax-free money for basic medical care, medical providers will compete for their dollars by offering the best service at the lowest price; and it will become much tougher for doctors, hospitals, and drug companies to jack up their costs without losing business.

According to America's Health Insurance Plans, a national association, 10 million Americans now possess HSA-eligible policies.[7] Rather than encourage this trend, however, Obamacare puts HSAs in leg irons. Come 2011, HSA funds may not purchase over-the-counter remedies.[8] Also, higher penalties will hit those who make non-medical withdrawals from their accounts.[9]

Rather than stymie Americans who want to save money to care for themselves (could anything be more responsible?), the federal government should deregulate HSAs and encourage Americans to use this tool to take charge of their own medical care.

5) Allow health insurance to be sold across state lines.

Americans may buy virtually anything they want from anyone in any state—but not health insurance. This insidious exception must end.

State-level medicrats harm consumers twice:

First, expensive state government regulations create wild, state-to-state cost disparities. A 25-year-old, male nonsmoker in Newark, New Jersey, for instance, would shell out $3,263 annually for the cheapest Preferred Provider Organization plan available via eHealthInsurance.com. But in Louisville, Kentucky, which imposes fewer rules, he would pay just $336 for equivalent coverage.

Second, these same state-level functionaries prevent that young Newark man from saving $2,927 by buying the same coverage from a Kentucky insurer. In essence, domestic protectionism shields costly New Jersey underwriters from outside competition.

If Congress tore down these internal tariff walls, Americans could shop nationwide for health insurance. This would make coverage more affordable for millions—and competition would push prices down for those already insured.[10]

6) Pry mandated benefits from health plans.

State-level (and soon federal) mandates for non-essential health benefits fuel higher prices. Forcing insurance plans to cover things like hair plugs, breast reduction, and *in vitro* fertilization increases coverage costs by 10.5 percent in the average state, according to a 2010 study by Pacific Research Institute scholar Benjamin Zycher.[11]

Likewise, car prices would climb if government required every vehicle to include a GPS system, seat warmers, and a sunroof. Eliminating such luxurious benefit mandates would reduce premiums significantly.[12]

Other regulations on insurance, like "community rating," similarly drive up prices. If the government forces insurers to charge everyone the same premium—never mind preexisting conditions, health status, or family history—everyone's premiums will increase.

7) Implement state lawsuit reform as part of health care reform.

Liberating doctors will require leashing lawyers.

Each year, one of every eight physicians can look forward to a lawsuit. Such litigation is justified when doctors behave negligently or recklessly, but the fact is 90 percent of doctors win their cases in court. These victories, however, come at a high price: legal bills typically approach $100,000 per case.[13] Even when they prevail, these doctors are victimized by a civil-justice system in which gurney-chasing lawyers sue multiple doctors in hopes that a rare courtroom triumph will yield the bonanza that compensates for so many more failed cases. Aside from legal harassment that doctors face, malpractice insurance can sometimes cost them $240,000 a year.[14]

Everyone's expenses soar when doctors feel compelled to practice "defensive medicine," essentially using every test and medical device invented since the tongue depressor—not because doing so makes therapeutic sense, but just so they can tell juries that they took every possible step to diagnose and treat patients who then turned around and sued them.

This mess costs America's medical system some $124 billion a year, according to a Pacific Research Institute study by Lawrence McQuillan and Hovannes Abramyan.[15]

Reforms that would help improve this situation include limiting payouts for "non-economic damages" (essentially "quality of life" damages, or damages to which an objective market price can't be put).

Just look at what's happened in Texas. In 2003, the Lone Star State instituted a $250,000 cap on non-economic damages. Prior to this reform, the state was a hotspot of medical malpractice litigation. Dallas County alone was home to 1,108 medical liability suits in 2003. The very next year, that number dropped to 142.[16]

In addition, malpractice cases should be heard by special, medically savvy health courts. Defendants who lose their cases should be allowed to pay damages in installments rather than lump sums. And we should curb excessive attorney's fees— particularly in obscene instances, such as when a relatively small group of lawyers pocketed $1.5 billion in fees, while their clients, patients who were found harmed by the drug Vioxx, saw less than $100,000 each.[17] If the fees earned by attorneys were limited to no more than four times (say) the damages paid to the harmed individuals, frivolous suits would end overnight.

8) Make doctors' charitable care tax-deductible.

The U.S. Tax Code should be changed to encourage doctors to provide as much charitable treatment as they care to deliver.

Imagine that Dr. Sheila Washington, MD, sees poor and uninsured patients for free, three hours each week. If Dr. Washington normally averages $150 an hour in her practice, she ought to be free to deduct $450 from her taxes each week that she performs this public service through her private initiative.

Instantly, doctors would find it far easier to treat low-income, uninsured patients. America would be far better off with as many doctors as possible donating their talents to the needy. Many would like to do this but feel they can't, given the economics of the current system.

9) Modernize Medicare.

Medicare should be turned into a patient-friendly, HSA-like program.

Rather than pay federal bureaucrats to manage every excruciating detail of this entitlement behemoth, the Medicare administration should place, say, $250,000 into an account from which each senior would purchase elder-care insurance. If the senior citizen outlives this money, Medicare would pay additional sums as necessary.

Doctors and hospitals seeking the business of such Medicare recipients would have to post prices at the point of service and online. This would help seniors and their caretakers shop for medical treatment, which, in turn, would control costs. Look at laser eye surgery. Price-conscious consumers have cut the cost of this surgery over the past decade from $2,200 per eye to $1,350.[18]

10) Let vouchers do the work.

The most cost-effective way for government to help poor people who are without health insurance, and who don't have any other options to get it, is simply to provide these people with $5,000 vouchers to buy the health insurance policy of their choice. That doesn't require a huge bureaucracy or a 2,400-page bill filled with innumerable new agencies and impenetrable new rules. All you need are people to process the applications and people to police the system for fraud—simple and effective.

These ten reforms would help the United States flip a U-turn and flee Obamacare with all deliberate speed. The alternative is for America to remain on the road to serfdom, which has no off-ramp.

ACKNOWLEDGEMENTS

Without the assistance and dedication of so many, this book would not have been possible. A special vote of thanks goes to Pacific Research Institute's vice president, marketing, Rowena Itchon, without whose tremendous commitment and tireless efforts, this book would not have been possible. I am also so appreciative of the efforts of the talented team at Keybridge Communications for their role. And, of course, the renowned health care scholars at PRI and around the nation who have made my work so much easier.

It was an honor to have been approached by Regnery Publishing to undertake this book project, *The Truth about Obamacare*. I extend my deepest thanks to Regnery for having the confidence in me to write this important book. Special thanks go to Jeff Carneal, president of Eagle Publishing, Marji Ross, president and publisher of Regnery, Harry Crocker, vice president and executive editor, Mary Beth Baker, managing editor, and Farahn Morgan, editorial assistant.

I am so very grateful to the supporters of the Pacific Research Institute who made it possible for me to undertake a project of this magnitude. Not only their financial support but their advice and encouragement of my efforts on health care are also invaluable to me.

In the end, any errors or omissions are my sole responsibility.

NOTES

INTRODUCTION

1. Associated Press, "It's the law of the land: Health overhaul signed," MSNBC, March 23, 2010; available at: http://www.msnbc.msn.com/id/35999823 [accessed June 4, 2010].

2. Martina Stewart, "Aide: Obama more excited by bill passing than being elected," CNN Political Ticker, March 22, 2010; available at: http://politicalticker.blogs.cnn.com/2010/03/22/aide-obama-more-excited-by-bill-passing-than-being-elected/?fbid=cm8kiKlegGg [accessed June 4, 2010].

3. "And with the strokes of 39 pens, a major expansion of health coverage," *Washington Post*, Paper Trail, April 19, 2010; available at: http://www.washingtonpost.com/wp-dyn/content/article/2010/04/15/AR2010041505460.html [accessed June 4, 2010].

4. "Barack Obama and Joe Biden's Plan to Lower Health Care Costs and Ensure Affordable, Accessible Health Coverage for All,"

BarackObama.com, http://www.barackobama.com/pdf/issues/
HealthCareFullPlan.pdf [accessed June 4, 2010].

5.   "A Politics of Conscience," BarackObama.com, June 23, 2007; avail-
       able at: http://www.barackobama.com/2007/06/23/a_politics_of_
       conscience_1.php [accessed June 4, 2010].

6.   "Barack Obama and Joe Biden's Plan to Lower Health Care Costs and
       Ensure Affordable, Accessible Health Coverage for All," *op. cit.*

7.   Ibid.

8.   Richard S. Foster, Chief Actuary Centers for Medicare and Medicaid,
       "Estimated Financial Effects of the 'Patient Protection and Afford-
       able Care Act,' as Amended"; available at: http://
       s3.amazonaws.com/thf_media/2010/pdf/OACT-Memo-FinImpac-
       tofPPACA-Enacted.pdf p.3

9.   Robert Pear and David M. Herszenhorn, "Obama Hails Vote on
       Health Care as Answering 'the Call of History,'" *New York Times*,
       March 21, 2010; available at: http://www.nytimes.com/2010/03/22/
       health/policy/22health.html [accessed June 4, 2010].

10.   Associated Press, "Report: Health overhaul will increase USA's tab,"
       USA Today, April 23, 2010; available at: http://www.usatoday.com/
       news/washington/2010-04-22-health-care-costs_N.htm [accessed
       June 4, 2010].

11.   T. M. Lindsey, "Obama's promise for health care reform comes full
       circle," *Iowa Independent*, March 25, 2010; available at: http://
       iowaindependent.com/30682/obama's-promise-for-health-care-
       reform-comes-full-circle.

CHAPTER 1

1.   Sandro Contenta, "Canadian health care has a dirty secret," *Global
       Post*, March 3, 2010; available at: http://www.globalpost.com/
       dispatch/canada/100302/health-care-danny-williams [accessed
       June 4, 2010].

2.   Understanding Rituxan Use in Canada, Lymphoma Foundation
       Canada, http://www.lymphoma.ca/rituxanfundingbyprovince.htm
       [accessed June 4, 2010].

3.   Associated Press, "Obama promises universal health care by end of
       first term," *Chicago Sun Times*, May 14, 2007; available at: http://

www.suntimes.com/news/elections/385287,051407obama.article [accessed June 14, 2010].

4. Scott Conroy, "Obama Unveils Universal Health Care Plan," CBS News, May 29, 2007; available at: http://www.cbsnews.com/stories/2007/05/29/politics/main2863074.shtml [accessed June 4, 2010].

5. Nick Kimball, "Stand for Change: Video of 1,000-person New Year's Eve Rally in Ames," BarackObama.com, January 1, 2008; available at: http://my.barackobama.com/page/community/tag/Ames [accessed June 4, 2010].

6. "Waiting your Turn," Hospital Waiting Lists in Canada, 2009 Report, October 2009; available at: http://gsa.lexi.net/search?q=cache:ccCGdXFGi4IJ:www.fraserinstitute.org/commerce.web/product_files/WaitingYourTurn_2009.pdf + hospital + waiting + lists + in + canada%3A + 2009 + report&site=fraser&client=fraser_frontend&access=p&ie=UTF-8&proxystylesheet=fraser_frontend&output=xml_no_dtd&oe=UTF-8 [accessed June 4, 2010].

7. Ibid.

8. Ibid.

9. "OECD Health Data 2009—comparing health statistics across OECD countries," PAC/COM/NEWS, July 3, 2009; available at: http://www.olis.oecd.org/olis/2009doc.nsf/ENGDATCORPLOOK/NT0000490A/$FILE/JT03267652.PDF, p. 3 [accessed June 4, 2010].

10. "OECD Health Data 2009—Frequently Requested Data," November 2009; Excel file available to download at: http://www.oecd.org/document/16/0,3343,en_2649_34631_2085200_1_1_1_1,00.html [accessed June 4, 2010].

11. Blanche Lincoln, "Man pulls out 13 of his own teeth with pliers 'because he couldn't find an NHS dentist,'" *Mail* online, February 6, 2009; available at: http://www.dailymail.co.uk/news/article-1135582/Man-pulls-13-teeth-pliers-NHS-dentist.html [accessed June 4, 2010].

12. Jenny Hope and Nick McDermott, "The babies born in hospital corridors: Bed shortage forces 4,000 mothers to give birth in lifts, offices and hospital toilets," *Daily Mail* online, August 26, 2009; available at: http://www.dailymail.co.uk/news/article-1209034/The-babies-born-hospital-corridors-Bed-shortage-forces-4-000-mothers-birth-lifts-offices-hospital-toilets.html [accessed June 4, 2010].

13. Kurt Loder, " 'Sicko': Heavily Doctored," MTV Movie review, June 29, 2007; available at: http://www.mtv.com/movies/news/articles/1563758/story.jhtml [accessed June 4, 2010].

14. "Government-run Health Care in England," DiscoverTheNetworks.org, http://www.discoverthenetworks.org/viewSubCategory.asp?id=621 [accessed June 4, 2010]. See also: "Towards greater partnership in healthcare funding: The rise of health consumerism in British and other European healthcare systems," Centre for the New Europe; available at: http://www.cne.org/pub_pdf/2004_09_00_uk_health.pdf [accessed June 4, 2010].

15. "Towards greater partnership in healthcare funding," *op. cit.*

16. Johnny Munkhammar, M.Sc., Timbro, "Are Markets and Health Care Compatible?"; available at: http://www.munkhammar.org/blog/pdf/MunkhammarGalenRemarks.doc [accessed June 4, 2010].

17. Sally C. Pipes, "Losing by 'Saving,'" *New York Post*, February 5, 2008; available at: http://www.nypost.com/seven/02052008/postopinion/opedcolumnists/losing_by_saving_841252.htm?page=2 [accessed June 4, 2010].

18. Ibid.

19. "NICE And Its Decision Not To Approve Rheumatoid Arthritis Drug Abatacept, UK," *Medical News Today*, May 5, 2008; available at: http://www.medicalnewstoday.com/articles/106184.php [accessed June 4, 2010].

20. "Tarceva approved in Europe for lung cancer," Roche, September 21, 2005; available at: http://www.roche.com/inv-update-2005-09-21 [accessed June 4, 2010].

21. Jenny Hope, "Lung cancer drug is banned in England because of its cost—but will be available to Scots," *Daily Mail* online, April 24, 2008; available at: http://www.dailymail.co.uk/health/article-561800/Lung-cancer-drug-banned-England-cost—available-Scots.html [accessed June 4, 2010].

22. Kate Devlin, "Expensive lung cancer drug to be available on the NHS," *UK Telegraph*, November 25, 2008; available at: http://www.telegraph.co.uk/health/healthnews/3521382/Expensive-lung-cancer-drug-to-be-available-on-the-NHS.html [accessed June 4, 2010].

23. David Gratzer, "American Cancer Care Beats the Rest," *Wall Street Journal*, July 22, 2008; available at: http://online.wsj.com/article/ SB121668625082172105.html?mod=googlenews_wsj [accessed June 4, 2010].

24. Devon Herrick, "FYI: We're Number One. Again!" John Goodman's Health Policy Blog, July 30, 2008; available at: http://www.john-goodman-blog.com/were-number-one-again/ [accessed June 4, 2008].

25. "Life Expectancy at All Time High; Death Rates Reach New Low, New Report Shows," CDC Online Newsroom, August 19, 2009; available at: http://www.cdc.gov/media/pressrel/2009/r090819.htm [accessed June 4, 2010].

26. Uniform Crime Reporting Program, Crime in the United States, 2005, Table 16, http://www.fbi.gov/ucr/05cius/data/table_16.html [accessed June 4, 2010].

27. "List of countries by intentional homicide rate," http:// en.wikipedia.org/wiki/List_of_countries_by_homicide_rate#cite_ note-winslow-interpol-pakistan-40 [accessed June 4, 2010]. (Further sources available on this page for each stat.)

28. Data available at: http://www-fars.nhtsa.dot.gov/Main/index.aspx [accessed June 4, 2010].

29. BigGovHealth, Myths and Facts, http://www.biggovhealth.org/ resource/myths-facts/ [accessed June 4, 2010].

30. "The Business of Health," American Enterprise Institute for Public Policy Research; available at: http://www.aei.org/publications/ pubID.24974,filter.all/pub_detail.asp (bios) [accessed June 4, 2010]. See also: http://ibdeditorials.com/IBDArticles.aspx?id= 270338135202343

31. Gregory Mankiw, "Beyond Those Health Care Numbers," *New York Times*, November 4, 2007; available at: http://www.nytimes.com/ 2007/11/04/business/04view.html?_r=2&adxnnl=1&oref=slogin& ref=business&adxnnlx=1217851257-7nWTn5MwZIt8rzpUMnTlBg [accessed June 4, 2010].

32. Geneva Foundation for Medical Education and Research, http:// www.gfmer.ch/Medical_education_En/Live_birth_definition.htm [accessed June 4, 2010].

33.   See http://www.genethique.org/en/letters/letters/2008/march.htm [accessed June 4, 2010]

34.   David Hogberg, Ph.D., "Don't Fall Prey to Propaganda: Life Expectancy and Infant Mortality are Unreliable Measures for Comparing the U.S. Health Care System to Others," National Policy Analysis, July 2006; available at: http://www.nationalcenter.org/ NPA547ComparativeHealth.html [accessed June 4, 2010].

35.   Bernardine Healy, "Behind the Baby Count," *US News & World Report*, September 24, 2006; available at: http://health.usnews.com/ usnews/health/articles/060924/2healy.htm [accessed June 4, 2010].

36.   Michelle Lang "Calgary's quads: Born in the U.S.A.," *Calgary Herald*, August 17, 2007; available at: http://www.canada.com/ calgaryherald/story.html?id=41ccae74-8325-449a-b89f-e68957ca25ae&k=79546 [accessed June 4, 2010].

37.   Glen Whitman, "Who's Fooling Who? The World Health Organization's Problematic Ranking of Health Care Systems," CATO Institute, February 28, 2008; available at: http://www.cato.org/pubs/bp/ bp101.pdf [accessed June 4, 2010].

38.   "World Health Organization Assesses the World's Health Systems," World Health Organization; available at: http://www.who.int/whr/ 2000/media_centre/press_release/en/index.html [accessed June 4, 2010].

39.   Information previously available at: http://www.ibdeditorials.com/ IBDArticles.aspx?id=299282509335931.

40.   Antonia Maioni, "The Castonguay Report: Quebec's Quiet Revolutionary Strikes Again," *The Health File*, April 2008; available at: http://www.irpp.org/po/archive/apr08/maioni.pdf [accessed June 4, 2010].

41.   "Unsocialized Medicine," *Wall Street Journal*, June 13, 2005; available at: http://www.opinionjournal.com/editorial/feature.html?id= 110006813 [accessed June 4, 2010].

42.   "Canadian Health Officials: Our Universal Health Care Is 'Sick,' Private Insurance Should Be Welcomed," FOX News, August 17, 2009; available at: http://www.foxnews.com/story/0,2933,539943,00.html [accessed June 4, 2010].

43. Richard Smith, "The private sector in the English NHS: from pariah to saviour in under a decade," *CMAJ*, August 2, 2005; available at: http://www.cmaj.ca/cgi/content/full/173/3/273 [accessed June 4, 2010].

44. Ibid.

CHAPTER 2

1. Sally C. Pipes, "The Top Myths of Health Care," speech at USC, April 12, 2010.

2. Sally C. Pipes, *Miracle Cure: How to Solve America's Health-Care Crisis and Why Canada Isn't the Answer* (Pacific Research Institute, 2004).

3. Milton Friedman, "How to Cure Health Care," *Public Interest*, Winter 2001; available at: http://www.thepublicinterest.com/archives/ 2001winter/article1.html [accessed June 7, 2010]. Abridged version available at: http://www.hoover.org/publications/digest/ 3459466.html [accessed June 7, 2010].

4. Sally C. Pipes, *Miracle Cure*.

5. David Gratzer, *The Cure: How Capitalism Can Save American Health Care* (New York: Encounter Books, 2006), 45.

6. David Gratzer, *The Cure: How Capitalism Can Save American Health Care*, 46

7. Ibid.

8. Sally C. Pipes, *Miracle Cure*.

9. Inflation adjusted.

10. David Gratzer, *The Cure*, 47.

11. Ibid., 50.

12. "State Children's Health Insurance Program (SCHIP): An Overview," *Washington Post*, October 17, 2007; available at: http://www. washingtonpost.com/wp-dyn/content/article/2007/10/17/ AR2007101702108.html [accessed June 7, 2010].

13. Ibid.

14. Milton Friedman, "How to Cure Health Care," *op. cit.*

15. Christopher Weaver, "Government Health Spending To Top Private Sector By 2012," *Kaiser Health News*, February 4, 2010; available at:

http://www.kaiserhealthnews.org/Stories/2010/February/04/cms-government-insurance.aspx [accessed June 7, 2010].

CHAPTER 3

1. "Yes President Obama, You did promise a public health plan," *Daily Kos*, December 23, 2009; available at: http://www.dailykos.com/story/2009/12/23/818495/-Yes-President-Obama,-You-did-promise-a-public-health-plan [accessed June 7, 2010].

2. "Obama Ripped Mrs. Clinton for Proposing a Health Care Mandate," *The Rush Limbaugh Show*, March 24, 2010; available at: http://www.rushlimbaugh.com/home/daily/site_032410/content/0 1125108.guest.html [accessed June 7, 2010].

3. Robert Pear, "Democrats Agree on a Health Plan; Now Comes the Hard Part," *New York Times*, March 31, 2009; available at: http://www.nytimes.com/2009/04/01/us/politics/01health.html [accessed June 7, 2010].

4. Carl Hulse and Jeff Zeleny, "Democrats Seem Set to Go It Alone on a Health Bill," *New York Times*, August 18, 2009; available at: http://www.nytimes.com/2009/08/19/health/policy/19repubs.html [accessed June 7, 2010].

5. Elizabeth Drew, "Is There Life in Health Care Reform?" *The New York Review of Books*, March 11, 2010; available at: http://www.nybooks.com/articles/archives/2010/mar/11/is-there-life-in-health-care-reform/ [accessed June 7, 2010].

6. Susan Davis, "WSJ/NBC News Poll: 46% Say Health Overhaul Is a Bad Idea," *Wall Street Journal*, January 19, 2010; available at: http://blogs.wsj.com/washwire/2010/01/19/wsjnbc-news-poll-46-say-health-overhaul-is-a-bad-idea/tab/article/ [accessed June 7, 2010].

7. Timothy P. Carney, "Obama gives sugar plums to the special interests," *Washington Examiner*, March 24, 2010; available at: http://www.washingtonexaminer.com/politics/Obama-gives-sugar-plums-to-the-special-interests-88958037.html [accessed June 7, 2010].

8. Ibid.

9. Ibid.

10. Grace-Marie Turner, "Promises Made—and Broken," National Review Online, November 2, 2009; available at: http://healthcare.nationalreview.com/post/ ?q=MGQ2NjA1MzM3NGNhNDc4OTg2ODIwNTRhY2JhNmZkMGM [accessed June 16, 2010].

11. Ibid.

12. Ibid.

13. Grace-Marie Turner, "Duplicity and Deceit," the Galen Institute, November 20, 2009; available at: http://www.galen.org/compo-nent,8/action,show_content/id,14/blog_id,1309/category_id,0/type ,33/ [accessed June 7, 2010].

14. Grace-Marie Turner, "Promises Made—and Broken," *op. cit.*

15. Ibid.

16. Carl Hulse and Robert Pear, "Sweeping Health Care Plan Passes House," *New York Times*, November 7, 2009; available at: http://www.nytimes.com/2009/11/08/health/policy/08health.html [accessed June 7, 2010].

17. "Obama on Fox Defends 'Louisiana Purchase,'" Newsmax.com, March 17, 2010; available at: http://www.newsmax.com/Inside-Cover/obama-healthcare-fox-interview/2010/03/17/id/353090 [accessed June 16, 2010].

18. Alan Silverleib, "Senate approves health care reform bill," CNN.com, December 24, 2009; available at: http://www.cnn.com/ 2009/POLITICS/12/24/health.care/index.html [accessed June 16, 2010].

19. http://en.wikipedia.org/wiki/Patient_Protection_and_ Affordable_Care_Act

20. Chip Reid, "Obama Reneges on Health Care Transparency," CBS News, January 6, 2010; available at: http://www.cbsnews.com/stories/ 2010/01/06/eveningnews/main6064298.shtml [accessed June 7, 2010].

21. Shailagh Murray and Lori Montgomery, "House Passes Healthcare Reform Bill without Republican Votes," Progressive Democrats of America, March 22, 2010; available at: http://www.pdamerica.org/ articles/news/2010-03-22-08-46-56-news.php [accessed June 16, 2010].

22. Peter Suderman, "Nancy Pelosi on Health Care: 'We have to pass the bill so that you can find out what is in it,'" *Reason*, March 9, 2010; available at: http://reason.com/blog/2010/03/09/nancy-pelosi-on-health-care-we [accessed June 16, 2010].

23. Rob Wells and Shayndi Raice, "Summary of Patient Protection And Affordable Care Act," Nasdaq; available at: http://www.nasdaq.com/aspx/stock-market-news-story.aspx?storyid=201003212306dowjonesdjonline000366&title=summary-of-patient-protection-and-affordable-care-act [accessed June 16, 2010].

24. Shailagh Murray and Lori Montgomery, "House Passes Healthcare Reform Bill without Republican Votes," *op. cit.*

25. Bill Frist, "A Historic and Dangerous Senate Mistake," *Wall Street Journal*, February 25, 2010; available at: http://online.wsj.com/article/SB10001424052748704479404575087163975017470.html?mod=googlenews_wsj [accessed June 7, 2010].

26. Ibid.

27. http://en.wikipedia.org/wiki/Patient_Protection_and_Affordable_Care_Act

28. Ibid.

29. Ibid.

30. Robert Pear, "Health Care Cost Increase Is Projected for New Law," *New York Times*, April 23, 2010; available at: http://www.nytimes.com/2010/04/24/health/policy/24health.html [accessed June 7, 2010].

31. Ibid.

32. Stephen Ohlemacher, "Nearly 4M To Pay Health Insurance Penalty By 2016," *The Bulletin*, April 25, 2010; available at: http://thebulletin.us/articles/2010/04/25/news/nation/doc4bd44fb223baf050842329.txt [accessed June 7, 2010].

33. Nicole Gaouette, Catherine Dodge, and Ryan J. Donmoyer, "Senate Passes Measure to Overhaul Health-Care System (Update6)," Bloomberg, December 24, 2009; available at: http://www.bloomberg.com/apps/news?pid=20601070&sid=aNx_RWtNhDkE [accessed June 7, 2010].

CHAPTER 4

1. David Whelan, "Obamacare Under Legal Siege," Forbes.com, The Science Business, April 9, 2010; available at: http://blogs.forbes.com/sciencebiz/2010/04/assault-on-Obamacare/ [accessed June 7, 2010].

2. Martin Vaughan, "IRS May Withhold Tax Refunds to Enforce Health-Care Law," *Wall Street Journal*, April 15, 2010; available at: http://online.wsj.com/article/SB10001424052702304510004575186082454662468.html?mod=WSJ_latestheadlines [accessed June 7, 2010].

3. Congressman Steve King, "Congressman Steve King Talks about Tax Day," *Right Side News*, April 20, 2010; available at: http://www.rightsidenews.com/201004209664/politics-and-economics/congressman-steve-king-talks-about-tax-day.html [accessed June 7, 2010].

4. Martin Vaughan, "IRS May Withhold Tax Refunds to Enforce Health-Care Law," *op. cit.*

5. The Henry J. Kaiser Family Foundation, "Summary of New Health Reform Law," April 8, 2010, page 1, Publication No. 8061; available at: http://www.kff.org/healthreform/8061.cfm [accessed June 7, 2010].

6. Richard S. Foster, Chief Actuary Centers for Medicare and Medicaid, "Estimated Financial Effects of the 'Patient Protection and Affordable Care Act,' as Amended"; available at: http://www.politico.com/static/PPM130_oact_memorandum_on_financial_impact_of_ppaca_as_enacted.html

7. U.S. Department of Health and Human Services, The 2009 HHS Poverty Guidelines, http://aspe.hhs.gov/poverty/09poverty.shtml.

8. Jill Jackson and John Nolen, "Health Care Reform Bill Summary: Look at What's in the Bill," CBSNews.com, March 23, 2010; available at: http://www.cbsnews.com/8301-503544_162-20000846-503544.html [accessed June 7, 2010].

9. Robert Pear, "Health Care Cost Increase is Projected for New Law," *op. cit.*

10. Tom Price, "159 New Government Agencies Won't Improve Health Care," Republican Study Committee, March 19, 2010; available at:

http://rsc.tomprice.house.gov/News/DocumentSingle.aspx? DocumentID=177348 [accessed June 7, 2010].

11.   Grace-Marie Turner, "Trying to 'Fix' the Costs of ObamaCare," *The Daily Caller*, April 22, 2010; available at: http://dailycaller.com/2010/04/22/trying-to-fix-the-costs-of-obamacare/ [accessed June 7, 2010].

12.   Martin Vaughan, "IRS May Withhold Tax Refunds to Enforce Health-Care Law," *op. cit.*

13.   Richard S. Foster, "Estimated Financial Effects of the 'Patient Protection and Affordable Care Act,' as Amended," *op. cit.*

14.   Douglas Elmendorf, Congressional Budget Office letter to House Speaker Nancy Pelosi, March 18, 2010, Table 2; available at: http://www.cbo.gov/ftpdocs/113xx/doc11355/hr4872.pdf.

CHAPTER 5

1.   "Breakdown of the Uninsured," James E. Risch, http://risch.senate.gov/public/?p=BreakdownoftheUninsured [accessed June 7, 2010].

2.   http://www.census.gov/Press-Release/www/releases/archives/income_wealth/014227.html

3.   "People Without Health Insurance by Selected Characteristics: 2007 and 2008" (Table 7), available at: http://www.census.gov/hhes/www/hlthins/hlthin08/hlthtables08.html.

4.   "The Uninsured in America," Blue Cross Blue Shield Association; available at: http://www.coverageforall.org/pdf/BC-BS_Uninsured-America.pdf [accessed June 7, 2010]; http://www.ncpa.org/pub/st/st269/st269b.htm

5.   "Breakdown of the Uninsured," James E. Risch, *op. cit.*

6.   "Slaughter Stands Up For Western New York at White House Health Care Summit," Congresswoman Louise M. Slaughter, February 25, 2010; available at: http://www.louise.house.gov/index.php?option=com_content&view=article&id=1475:slaughter-stands-up-for-western-new-york-at-white-house-health-care-summit&catid=91:press-releases-2010&Itemid=141 [accessed June 7, 2010].

7.   "Income, Poverty and Health Insurance in the United States: 2008," http://www.census.gov/hhes/www/income/income08.html.

8. "People Without Health Insurance by Selected Characteristics: 2007 and 2008" (Table 7), available at: http://www.census.gov/hhes/ www/hlthins/hlthin08/hlthtables08.html

9. Ibid.

10. Ibid.

11. From Sally Pipes, Myth 3, in *The Top Ten Myths of American Health Care* (Pacific Research Institute, 2008), 35.

12. "Breakdown of the Uninsured," James E. Risch, *op. cit.*

13. Bernadette D. Proctor, Carmen DeNavas-Walt, and Jessica C. Smith, "Income, Poverty, and Health Insurance Coverage in the United States: 2008," Current Population Reports, U.S. Census Bureau, September 2009; available at: http://www.census.gov/prod/2009pubs/ p60-236.pdf [accessed June 17, 2010].

14. David Gratzer, "What Health Insurance Crisis?" *Los Angeles Times*, August 29, 2004; available at: http://www.manhattan-institute.org/ html/_lat-imes-what_health.htm [accessed June 7, 2010].

15. Ibid.

16. Amy J. Davidoff, Bowen Garrett, and Alshadye Yemane, "Medicaid-Eligible Adults Who Are Not Enrolled: Who Are They and Do They Get the Care They Need?" Urban Institute, Series A, No. A-48, October 2001; available at: http://www.urban.org/publications/ 310378.html [accessed June 7, 2010].

17. "Reaching Eligible but Uninsured Children in Medicaid and SCHIP" (Washington DC: Georgetown University Health Policy Institute, Center for Children and Families, March, 2008); available at: http:// ccf.georgetown.edu/index/reaching-eligible-but-uninsured-children [accessed June 7, 2010].

18. Sally Pipes, Myth 3, in *The Top Ten Myths of American Health Care, op. cit.*

19. "Number of those without health insurance about 46 million," PolitiFact; available at: http://www.politifact.com/truth-o-meter/ statements/2009/aug/18/barack-obama/number-those-without-health-insurance-about-46-mil/ [accessed June 7, 2010].

20. Sally Pipes, *The Top Ten Myths of American Health Care*, 40.

21. http://www.census.gov/hhes/www/hlthins/hlthin08/p60no236_ table7.pdf

CHAPTER 6

1. "Healthcare Costs Around the World," Visual Economics, http:// www.visualeconomics.com/healthcare-costs-around-the-world_ 2010-03-01/ [accessed June 7, 2010].

2. "How The Average U.S. Consumer Spends Their Paycheck," Visual Economics, http://www.visualeconomics.com/how-the-average-us-consumer-spends-their-paycheck/ [accessed June 7, 2010].

3. NHE Web Tables, http://www.cms.gov/NationalHealthExpendData/ 02_NationalHealthAccountsHistorical.asp#TopOfPage [accessed June 7, 2010].

4. Ibid.

5. "What Are the Key Statistics for Breast Cancer?" American Cancer Society, September 18, 2009; available at: http://www.cancer.org/ docroot/CRI/content/CRI_2_4_1X_What_are_the_key_statistics_ for_breast_cancer_5.asp?sitearea [accessed June 7, 2010].

6. "How Is Breast Cancer Staged?" American Cancer Society, September 18, 2009; available at: http://www.cancer.org/docroot/CRI/ content/CRI_2_4_3X_How_is_breast_cancer_staged_5.asp?rnav=cri [accessed June 7, 2010].

7. David Gratzer, *The Cure*, 13.

8. Ibid., 14.

9. Ibid., 16.

10. "Tests show Cheney suffered 'mild heart attack,'" *USA Today*, The Oval, February 23, 2010; available at: http://content.usatoday.com/ communities/theoval/post/2010/02/tests-show-cheney-suffered-mild-heart-attack-/1 [accessed June 7, 2010].

11. David Gratzer, *The Cure*, 19.

12. "Heart Disease and Stroke Statistics," American Heart Association, http://www.americanheart.org/presenter.jhtml?identifier=3000090 [accessed June 7, 2010].

13. William L. O'Neill, *American High: The Years of Confidence, 1945–1960* (New York: Simon and Schuster, 1989).

14. David Gratzer, *The Cure*, 21.

15. Steve Sternberg, "Higher price for defibrillator implants," *USA Today*, June 25, 2006; available at: http://www.usatoday.com/news/health/2006-06-25-

defibrillators_x.htm [accessed June 17, 2010]. Note: According to *USA Today*, "Without complications, the average cost of having a defibrillator implanted is $42,184." Many online support groups peg the cost at sometimes over $100,000. (See, e.g.: http://www.icdsupportgroup.org/board/viewtopic.php?f=1&t=5039, and http://www.inspire.com/Twndd/journal/cost-of-icds/.)

16. David Gratzer, *The Cure*, 21.

17. Report on Conference "Medical Innovation in the Changing Healthcare Marketplace," held June 14 to 15, 2001, Washington, D.C., at the National Academy of Sciences; available at: http://www.nap.edu/openbook.php?record_id=10358&page=1 [accessed June 7, 2010].

18. Sally Pipes, *The Top Ten Myths of American Health Care*, 25.

19. "Births, Marriages, Divorces, and Deaths: Provisional Data for July 2009," *National Vital Statistics Report*, Vol. 58, Number 15; available at: http://www.cdc.gov/nchs/data/nvsr/nvsr58/nvsr58_15.htm [accessed June 7, 2010].

20. Table 290F: Deaths for Approximately 64 Selected Causes, by 10-Year Age Groups, Race, and Sex: United States, 1950-59; table available at: http://www.cdc.gov/nchs/data/dvs/dx1950_59.pdf [accessed June 7, 2010]. (TOTAL DEATHS IN 1950 = 1,452,454.) See also: Historical U.S. Population Growth by year 1900-1998, http://www.npg.org/facts/us_historical_pops.htm (TOTAL POPULATION IN 1950 = 152,271,417).

21. Life Expectancy—United States, Data 360, http://www.data360.org/dsg.aspx?Data_Set_Group_Id=195 [accessed June 7, 2010].

22. Craig Garthwaite, "Economic Benefits of Medical Innovations," Department of Management and Strategy, Kellogg School of Management, September 2009; available at: http://www.kellogg.northwestern.edu/faculty/garthwaite/htm/medical_innovations_garthwaite.pdf, p. 4.

23. Ibid., 33.

24. Mark Duggan & William Evans, 2008, "Estimating the Impact of Medical Innovation: A Case Study of HIV Antiretroviral Treatments," Forum for Health Economics & Policy, Berkeley Electronic Press, vol. 11(2), p. 1102; abstract available at: http://ideas.repec.org/p/nbr/nberwo/11109.html [accessed June 7, 2010].

25. Ibid.

26. Report on Conference "Medical Innovation in the Changing Health-care Marketplace," *op. cit.*, p. 4.

27. Gary S. Becker, "Health as human capital: synthesis and extensions," *Oxford Economic Papers* 59 (2007), 379–410 (Oxford University Press 2007); available at: http://oep.oxfordjournals.org/content/59/3/379.extract [accessed June 7, 2010].

28. *Consumer Expenditure Survey*, 2008, Table 47: Age of reference person: Shares of average annual expenditure and sources of income, ftp://ftp.bls.gov/pub/special.requests/ce/share/2008/age.txt [accessed June 7, 2010].

29. Ibid.

30. *Consumer Expenditure Survey*, 1989, Table 1300: Age of reference person: Shares of average annual expenditures and characteristics, ftp://ftp.bls.gov/pub/special.requests/ce/share/1989/age.txt [accessed June 7, 2010].

31. *Consumer Expenditure Survey*, 1999, Table 47: Age of reference person: Shares of average annual expenditures and sources of income, ftp://ftp.bls.gov/pub/special.requests/ce/share/1999/age.txt [accessed June 7, 2010].

32. *Consumer Expenditure Survey*, 2003, Table 47: Age of reference person: Shares of average annual expenditures and sources of income, ftp://ftp.bls.gov/pub/special.requests/ce/share/2003/age.txt [accessed June 7, 2010].

33. "Barack Obama on Health Care," On The Issues, http://www.ontheissues.org/Celeb/Barack_Obama_Health_Care.htm [accessed June 7, 2010].

34. "Fact Checking Obama's Speech," FactCheck.org, February 25, 2009; available at: http://www.factcheck.org/2009/02/fact-checking-obamas-speech/ [accessed June 7, 2010].

35. "Barack Obama on Health Care, On The Issues, *op. cit.*

36. "Health Insurance and Bankruptcy Rates in Canada and the United States," *Fraser Alert*, July 2009; available at: http://www.fraserinstitute.org/commerce.web/product_files/HealthInsuranceandBankruptcyRates.pdf [accessed June 7, 2010].

CHAPTER 7

1. Roni Caryn Rabin, "With Expanded Coverage for the Poor, Fears of a Big Headache," *New York Times*, April 26, 2010; available at: http://www.nytimes.com/2010/04/27/health/27landscape.html [accessed June 8, 2010].

2. Letter from Cindy Mann, Director Center for Medicaid and State Operations, CMS, April 9, 2010; available at: http://www.cms.gov/smdl/downloads/SMD10005.PDF [accessed June 8, 2010].

3. Roni Caryn Rabin, "With Expanded Coverage for the Poor, Fears of a Big Headache," *op. cit.*

4. Bernadette D. Proctor, et al., "Income, Poverty, and Health Insurance Coverage in the United States: 2008," *op. cit.*

5. "CMS Confirms ObamaCare Will Increase Spending," GOP.gov, *Policy News*, September 10, 2009; available at: http://www.gop.gov/policy-news/10/04/23/cms-confirms-Obamacare-will-increase [accessed June 8, 2010].

6. "Poverty: 2008 Highlights," U.S. Census Bureau, http://www.census.gov/hhes/www/poverty/poverty08/pov08hi.html [accessed June 8, 2010].

7. Data available at the Department of Health and Human Services, http://www.whitehouse.gov/omb/rewrite/budget/fy2008/hhs.html [accessed June 8, 2010].

8. Ibid.

9. John O'Shea, MD, "More Medicaid Means Less Quality Health Care," the Heritage Foundation, March 21, 2007; available at: http://www.heritage.org/Research/Reports/2007/03/More-Medicaid-Means-Less-Quality-Health-Care [accessed June 8, 2010].

10. "State Medicaid Prescription Drug Practices Linked to Worse Outcomes For Patients With Mental Illness," *Medical News Today*, May 4, 2009; available at: http://www.medicalnewstoday.com/articles/148694.php [accessed June 8, 2010].

11. Kevin Sack and Robert Pear, "States Consider Medicaid Cuts as Use Grows," *New York Times*, February 18, 2010; available at: http://www.nytimes.com/2010/02/19/us/politics/19medicaid.html [accessed June 8, 2010].

12. Kevin Sack, "As Medicaid Payments Shrink, Patients Are Abandoned," *New York Times*, March 15, 2010; available at: http://www.nytimes.com/2010/03/16/health/policy/16medicaid.html [accessed June 8, 2010].

13. "Report: Equal Pay for Equal Work? Not for Medicaid Doctors," HRG Publication #1822, *Public Citizen*, 2010; available at: http://www.citizen.org/publications/publicationredirect.cfm?ID=7541 [accessed June 8, 2010].

14. Jason Roberson, "Medicaid patients have trouble finding doctors in Dallas area," *The Dallas Morning News*, June 3, 2009; available at: http://www.dallasnews.com/sharedcontent/dws/bus/stories/060309dnbusmedicaid.4187740.html [accessed June 8, 2010].

15. Emily Ramshaw, "Keeping Their Bottom Lines Healthy," *The Texas Tribune*, May 5, 2010; available at: http://www.texastribune.org/stories/2010/may/05/doctor-dropout/ [accessed June 8, 2010].

16. Statesman Staff, "Some Idahoans can't find doctors," *Idaho Statesman*, March 16, 2010; available at: http://www.idahostatesman.com/2010/3/16/1118842/some-idahoans-cant-find-doctors.html?storylink=mirelated [accessed June 17, 2010].

17. "A Snapshot of U.S. Physicians: Key Findings from the 2008 Health Tracking Study Physician Survey," Center for Studying Health System Change, Data Bulletin No. 35, September 2009; available at: http://www.hschange.com/CONTENT/1078/?words=Medicaid + physicians#table4a [accessed June 8, 2010].

18. Tamyra Carroll Garcia, Amy B. Bernstein, and Mary Ann Bush, "Emergeny Department Visitors and Visits: Who Used the Emergency Room in 2007?" NCHS Data Brief, No. 38, May 2010; available at: http://www.cdc.gov/nchs/data/databriefs/db38.pdf [accessed June 8, 2010].

19. Mary Brophy Marcus, "Study: Uninsured don't go to the ER more than insured," *USA Today*, May 19, 2010; available at: http://www.usatoday.com/news/health/2010-05-20-emergency20_st_N.htm?loc=interstitialskip [accessed June 8, 2010].

20. Underpayment by Medicare and Medicaid Fact Sheet, American Hospital Association, November 2009; available at: http://www.

ihatoday.org/issues/payment/charity/underpymt.pdf [accessed June 8, 2010].

21. A. Dobson, J. DaVanzo, and N. Sen, "The Cost-Shift Payment 'Hydraulic': Foundation, History, and Implications," *Health Affairs*, Jan./Feb. 2006, 22–23; available at: http://content.healthaffairs.org/ cgi/content/full/25/1/22 [accessed June 17, 2010].

22. Underpayment by Medicare and Medicaid Fact Sheet, *op. cit.*

23. A. Dobson, et al., "The Cost-Shift Payment 'Hydraulic,'" *op. cit.*

24. Milliman, "Hospital & Physician Cost Shift: Payment Level Comparison of Medicare, Medicaid, and Commercial Players," Report presented by Will Fox and John Pickering, December 2008; available at: http://publications.milliman.com/research/health-rr/pdfs/ hospital-physician-cost-shift-RR12-01-08.pdf [accessed June 8, 2010].

25. Ibid.

26. "Medicaid's Continuing Crunch in a Recession: A Mid-Year Update for State FY 2010 and Preview for FY 2011," The Kaiser Commission on Medicaid and the Uninsured, http://www.kff.org/medicaid/ 8049.cfm [accessed June 8, 2010].

27. Ibid.

28. Ibid.

29. "State Medicaid Expenditures (in millions), SFY2008," http://www. statehealthfacts.org/comparemaptable.jsp?ind=186&cat=4 [accessed June 8, 2010].

30. "Health Care Reform, Medicaid and State Budget Woes," State Budget Solutions, March 24, 2010; available at: http://www. statebudgetsolutions.org/publications/detail/health-care-reform- medicaid-and-state-budget-woes [accessed June 8, 2010].

31. "Medicaid: Intergovernmental Transfers Have Facilitated State Financing Schemes," Statement of Kathryn G. Allen, Director, Health Care—Medicaid and Private Health Insurance Issues, March 18, 2004; available at: http://www.gao.gov/new.items/d04574t.pdf [accessed June 8, 2010].

32. Keith L. Martin, "Owner of New Jersey counseling center charged with Medicaid fraud," Insurance & Financial Advisor, May 14, 2010; available at: http://ifawebnews.com/2010/05/14/owner-of-new-

jersey-counseling-center-charged-with-medicaid-fraud/ [accessed June 8, 2010].

33. "Home of North Jersey healthcare exec raided in $5m Medicaid fraud case," *Jackson Online*, April 30, 2010; available at: http://www.jacksonnjonline.com/2010/04/30/home-of-north-jersey-healthcare-exec-raided-in-5m-medicaid-fraud-case/ [accessed June 8, 2010].

34. Thomas Cheplick, "Pennsylvania Medicaid Fraud Shows System Flaws," the Heartland Institute, May 1, 2009; available at: http://www.heartland.org/publications/health%20care/article/25001/Pennsylvania_Medicaid_Fraud_Shows_System_Flaws.html [accessed June 8, 2010].

35. Annie Linskey, "Bill could save state millions in Medicaid fraud," *The Baltimore Sun*, March 23, 2010; available at: http://articles.baltimoresun.com/2010-03-23/news/bal-md.fraud23mar23_1_medicaid-fraud-health-insurance-fraud-cases [accessed June 8, 2010].

36. Andrew Villegas, "How Fighting Health Fraud Is Like Playing Whack-A-Mole," NPR, May 13, 2010; available at: http://www.npr.org/blogs/health/2010/05/13/126802714/how-fighting-medical-fraud-is-like-whack-a-mole [accessed June 8, 2010].

37. Sally Pipes, Myth 8 in *The Top Ten Myths of American Health Care, op. cit.*

38. Andrew Villegas, "How Fighting Health Fraud Is Like Playing Whack-A-Mole," *op. cit.*

39. Medicaid Estate Planning: Gifting, Gross Estate, Estate Taxes for Senior Medicaid Asset Protection, Estate Street Partners, LLC, http://www.ultratrust.com/medicaid-estate-planning.html [accessed June 8, 2010].

CHAPTER 8

1. Remarks at Democratic presidential primary debate, CNN Election Center 2008, January 31, 2008; transcript available at: http://www.cnn.com/2008/POLITICS/01/31/dem.debate.transcript/index.html [accessed June 8, 2010].

2. *Health Care and Education Affordability Reconciliation Act of 2010*, HR 4872, 111th Cong., 2d sess. (January 5, 2010), Section 1002(a)

(pp. 8–9) as enacted; available at: http://www.opencongress.org/
bill/111-h4872/text [accessed June 8, 2010].

3. Congressional Budget Office, "Letter to Honorable Nancy Pelosi
regarding the effects of H.R. 3590 and H.R. 4872," March 20, 2010;
available at: http://cbo.gov/ftpdocs/113xx/doc11379/
Manager%27sAmendmenttoReconciliationProposal.pdf, p. 11.

4. House Ways and Means Committee Republican staff report, "The
Wrong Prescription: Democrats' Health Overhaul Dangerously
Expands IRS Authority," March 18, 2010; available at: http://
republicans.waysandmeans.house.gov/News/
DocumentSingle.aspx?DocumentID=176997 [accessed June 8, 2010].

5. "People Without Health Insurance by Selected Characteristics: 2007
and 2008" (Table 7), available at: http://www.census.gov/hhes/
www/hlthins/hlthin08/hlthtables08.html

6. "Government Responds to Health Care Reform Lawsuit," Planspon-
sor, May 13, 2010; available at: http://www.plansponsor.com/
Government_Responds_to_Health_Care_Reform_Lawsuit.aspx
[accessed June 8, 2010].

7. Randy E. Barnett, "The Insurance Mandate in Peril," *The Wall Street
Journal*, April 29, 2010; available at: http://online.wsj.com/article/
SB10001424052748704446704575206502199257916.html [accessed
June 8, 2010].

8. Igor Volsky, "Report: 411 States Rebel Over Health Care Reform Law,"
The Wonk Room, May 6, 2010; available at: http://
wonkroom.thinkprogress.org/2010/05/06/rebel-states-map/
[accessed June 8, 2010].

9. Associated Press, "Small Businesses Challenge Health Care Law," CBS
News, May 14, 2010; available at: http://www.cbsnews.com/stories/
2010/05/14/politics/main6482208.shtml [accessed June 8, 2010].

10. "Justice Needs More Time," *Wall Street Journal*, June 3, 2010; available at: http://online.wsj.com/article/SB1000142405274
8704596504575272882527805408.html [accessed June 17, 2010].

11. Health Insurance Requirements in Massachusetts, http://www.
massresources.org/infopages.cfm?ABPageID=93&MainParentID=93
[accessed June 8, 2010].

12. Robert Steinbrook, "Health Care Reform in Massachusetts—Expanding Coverage, Escalating Costs," *New England Journal of Medicine*, Volume 358:2757–60, June 26, 2008, Number 26; available at: http://content.nejm.org/cgi/content/full/358/26/2757 [accessed June 8, 2010].

13. Ibid.

14. Ibid.

15. Ibid.

16. Ibid.

17. Steven Malanga, "Health Care Reform: Welcome to NY, America," Real Clear Markets, March 24, 2010; available at: http://www.realclearmarkets.com/articles/2010/03/24/health_care_reform_welcome_to_ny_america_98390.html [accessed June 8, 2010].

18. Ibid.

19. Kay Lazar, "Short-term customers boosting health costs," *Boston Globe*, April 4, 2010; available at: http://www.boston.com/news/local/massachusetts/articles/2010/04/04/short_term_customers_boosting_health_costs/ [accessed June 8, 2010].

20. Ibid.

21. "The Massachusetts Insurance Blackout," *Wall Street Journal*, April 9, 2010; available at: http://online.wsj.com/article/SB10001424052702304198004575171782805022028.html [accessed June 8, 2010].

22. Ibid.

23. "Mass. insurers fault Gov. Deval Patrick for loss of revenue," *Boston Herald*, May 17, 2010; available at: http://www.bostonherald.com/business/health care/view.bg?articleid=1255468 [accessed June 17, 2010].

24. "The Massachusetts Insurance Blackout," *op. cit.*

25. Ibid.

26. Liz Kowalczyk, "Insurers may slash rates to hospitals," *Boston Globe*, May 24, 2010; available at: http://www.boston.com/yourtown/lynn/articles/2010/05/24/insurers_aim_to_cut_payments_to_hospitals_doctors_groups/ [accessed June 8, 2010].

27. Ibid.

28. Ibid.

29. Sally C. Pipes, "MAss Disaster," Op-Ed, Forbes.com, July 29, 2009; available at: http://www.forbes.com/2009/07/29/health-reform-massachusetts-opinions-contributors-obama-insurance.html [accessed June 8, 2010].

30. Liz Kowalczyk, "Insurers may slash rates to hospitals," *op. cit.*

31. Timothy P. Cahill, "Massachusetts Is Our Future," *Wall Street Journal*, March 25, 2010; available at: http://online.wsj.com/article/SB10001424052748704094104575144372942933394.html [accessed June 8, 2010].

32. Ibid.

33. My calculation, based on four years between implementation and now.

34. Conrad F. Meier, "Destroying Insurance Markets: How Guaranteed Issue and Community Rating Destroyed the Individual Health Insurance Market in Eight States," The Council for Affordable Health Insurance and The Heartland Institute, 2005; available at: http://www.cahi.org/cahi_contents/resources/pdf/destroyinginsmrkts05.pdf [accessed June 8, 2010].

35. Ibid.

36. Ibid.

37. "Maine's Dirigo Health: A String of Broken Promises," The Council for Affordable Health Insurance's Issues & Answers, January 2006, No. 132; available at: http://www.cahi.org/cahi_contents/resources/pdf/n132dirigo.pdf [accessed June 8, 2010].

38. "No Maine Miracle Cure," *Wall Street Journal*, August 21, 2009; available at: http://online.wsj.com/article/SB10001424052970204619004574322401816501182.html [accessed June 8, 2010].

39. Ibid.

CHAPTER 9

1. "State Health Benefit Mandates Increase the Number of Uninsured," Pacific Research Institute, July 1, 2008; available at: http://liberty.pacificresearch.org/press/state-health-benefit-mandates-increase-the-number-of-uninsured [accessed June 8, 2010].

2. Ibid.

3.   Victoria Craig Bunce, "Health Insurance Mandates in the States
      2009," Council for Affordable Health Insurance; available at: http://
      www.cahi.org/cahi_contents/resources/pdf/. HealthInsuranceMan-
      dates2009.pdf [accessed June 8, 2010].

4.   Sally C. Pipes, *The Top Ten Myths of American Health Care* (San
      Francisco: Pacific Research Institute); available at: http://www.
      pacificresearch.org/docLib/20081020_Top_Ten_Myths.pdf
      [accessed June 8, 2010].

5.   "New health insurance mandates would increase premiums," Keith-
      Hennessy.com, July 23, 2009; available at: http://keithhennessey.com/
      2009/07/23/higher-premiums/ [accessed June 8, 2010].

6.   Victoria Craig Bunce, "Health Insurance Mandates in the States
      2009," Council for Affordable Health Insurance, *op. cit.*

7.   Benjamin Zycher, "'Entrepreneurs' Coverage': An Alternative Health
      Policy Reform" (San Francisco: Pacific Research Institute, January
      2010), 27.

8.   Ibid.

9.   Ibid., 29.

10.   Victoria Craig Bunce, "Health Insurance Mandates in the States
      2009," *op. cit.*

11.   Patient Protection and Affordable Care Act, (Engrossed Amendment
      as Agreed to by Senate), H.R. 3590, 111th Cong. (2009); available at:
      http://www.cbsnews.com/htdocs/pdf/Senate_health_care_bill.pdf,
      Section 2713.

12.   Ibid., Section 1302.

13.   Ibid., Section 2711.

14.   Ibid., Section 2714.

15.   John R. Graham, "Meet the New Boss, Same As the Old Boss: Presi-
      dent Obama's Best Health 'Insurance' Reforms Were Passed in 1997,"
      Health Policy Prescriptions, Vol. 7, No. 9, September 2009, Pacific
      Research Institute; available at: http://www.pacificresearch.org/
      docLib/20090908_HPPv7n09_0909.pdf [accessed June 8, 2010].

CHAPTER 10

1.   Diane Stafford, "Employer-based health coverage is most widely
      used plan now but may not be in future," KansasCity.com, May 24,

2010; available at: http://economy.kansascity.com/?q=node/7247 [accessed June 8, 2010].

2. "Section-by-Section Analysis with Changes Made by Title X and Rec- onciliation included within Titles I–IX," The Patient Protection and Affordable Care Act; available at: http://dpc.senate.gov/. healthreformbill/healthbill96.pdf, p. 14 [accessed June 8, 2010].

3. Kurt L. P. Lawson, et al., "The employer health insurance 'mandate,'" Hogan Lovells, May 11, 2010; available at: http://www.lexology.com/ library/detail.aspx?g=3c72d03e-cf20-4b42-bd17-4976e0ffa5b1 [accessed June 8, 2010].

4. Devon Herrick and Pamela Villarreal, "Obama's Tax on Job Creation," National Center for Policy Analysis, May 18, 2010; available at: http://www.ncpa.org/pub/ba703 [accessed June 8, 2010].

5. Ibid.

6. Steve LeBlanc, "Small Businesses Fret Over Details Of Health Law," Associated Press, March 31, 2010; cited in RNC Research Briefing, Health Care Pulse Check, "Job Creators, Large And Small, Start Plan- ning Layoffs And Warn Customers Of Higher Prices To Come," March 31, 2010; available at: http://www.gop.com/index.php/ briefing/comments/health_care_pulse_check_-_job_creators_ planning_layoffs/ [accessed June 8, 2010].

7. Ibid.

8. "Summary—Health care bill signed on March 23, 2010," http:// www.njfb.org/newsletters/Health careSUMMARY.pdf [accessed June 17, 2010].

9. Devon Herrick and Pamela Villarreal, "Obama's Tax on Job Creation," *op. cit.*

CHAPTER 11

1. Federal Employees Health Benefits Program Handbook, http://opm. gov/insure/health/reference/handbook/fehb01.asp [accessed June 8, 2010].

2. Michael D. Tanner, "FEHBP Plan Is No 'Moderate Compromise,'" Cato @ Liberty, December 9, 2009; available at: http://www.cato-at- liberty.org/2009/12/09/fehbp-plan-is-no-moderate-compromise/ [accessed June 8, 2010].

3. Odin Anderson and Joel May, "The Federal Employees Health Benefits Program, 1961-1968: A Model for National Health Insurance?" in *Perspectives* (Chicago: Center for Health Administration Studies, University of Chicago).

4. Alain C. Enthoven, "The History and Principles of Managed Competition"; available at: http://content.healthaffairs.org/cgi/reprint/12/suppl_1/24 [accessed June 8, 2010].

5. "Overview of Open Access to Government Employee Program," http://www.randcompare.org/policy-options/open-access-to-government-employee-program [accessed June 8, 2010].

6. John C. Goodman and Gerald L. Musgrave, *A Primer on Managed Competition*, NCPA Policy Report No. 183, April 19, 1994; available at: http://www.ncpa.org/pdfs/st183.pdf [accessed June 8, 2010].

7. Jonathan Oberlander, Ph.D., "The Partisan Divide—The McCain and Obama Plans for U.S. Health Care Reform," *New England Journal of Medicine*, Vol. 359:781-784, No. 8, August 21, 2008; available at: http://content.nejm.org/cgi/content/full/359/8/781 [accessed June 8, 2010].

8. Peter Grier, "Health care reform bill 101: What's a health 'exchange'?" *Christian Science Monitor*, March 20, 2010; available at: http://www.csmonitor.com/USA/Politics/2010/0320/Health-care-reform-bill-101-What-s-a-health-exchange [accessed June 8, 2010]. "The federal government would provide states with start-up money for exchange establishment. The exchanges are supposed to be open for business by 2014. If a state declines to open one, Uncle Sam can step in and open an exchange himself."

9. *An Act to amend the Internal Revenue Code of 1986 to modify the first-time homebuyers credit in the case of members of the Armed Forces and certain other Federal employees, and for other purposes*, HR 3590, 111th Cong., 1st sess. (December 24, 2009); available at: http://www.cbsnews.com/htdocs/pdf/Senate_health_care_bill.pdf.

10. Victoria Craig Bunce, "Health Insurance Mandates in the States 2009," *op. cit.*

11. Robert Pear, "Senate Bill Sets a Plan to Regulate Premiums," *New York Times*, Aril 20, 2010; available at: http://www.nytimes.com/2010/04/21/health/policy/21health.html [accessed June 8, 2010].

12. Joshua Rhett Miller, "Unanswered Questions Abound on Health Insurance Exchanges," FOX News, March 25, 2010; available at: http://www.foxnews.com/politics/2010/03/25/unanswered-questions-abound-health-insurance-exchanges/ [accessed June 8, 2010]. To be successful, Solomon said, the exchanges should limit the number and variety of plans and require each insurer to cover a wide range of people with varying levels of health costs.

13. *America's Affordable Health Choices Act of 2009*, HR 3200, 111th Cong. (2009) (as reported in House); available at: http://www.opencongress.org/bill/111-h3200/text?version=rh&nid=t0:rh:163 [accessed June 8, 2010].

14. *Patient Protection and Affordable Care Act* (Engrossed Amendment as Agreed to by Senate), HR 3590, 111th Cong., 2d sess. (2009), Section 1101.

15. David S. Hilzenrath, "18 states refuse to run insurance pools for those with preexisting conditions," *Washington Post*, May 4, 2010; available at: http://www.washingtonpost.com/wp-dyn/content/article/2010/05/03/AR2010050304072.html [accessed June 8, 2010].

16. Alison Young, "New health care law traps some in pricey state plans," *USA Today*, April 29, 2010; available at: http://www.usatoday.com/news/health/2010-04-29-health-care-law-undercuts-risk-pools_N.htm [accessed June 8, 2010].

17. "Low-Cost Coverage In Obama Health Plan Not For All," Insurance-NewsNet.com, April 16, 2010; available at: http://insurancenews-net.com/article.aspx?id=180499&type=all [accessed June 17, 2010].

18. Grace-Marie Turner, "States Face Their First ObamaCare Test," *Wall Street Journal*, April 29, 2010; available at: http://online.wsj.com/article/SB10001424052748704471204575210180628430268.html?mod=WSJ_Opinion_LEFTTopOpinion [accessed June 8, 2010].

19. Mark Merlis, "Health Coverage for the High-Risk Uninsured: Policy Options for Design of the Temporary High-Risk Pool," Policy Analysis, No. 2, May 2010, National Institute for Health Care Reform; available at: http://www.nihcr.org/High-RiskPools.html [accessed June 17, 2010].

20. Report, "An Analysis of Health Insurance Premiums Under the Patient Protection and Affordable Care Act," Congressional Budget

Office, November 30, 2009; available at: http://www.cbo.gov/ftpdocs/107xx/doc10781/11-30-Premiums.pdf [accessed June 8, 2010]. "CBO and JCT estimate that the average premium per person covered (including dependents) for new nongroup policies would be about 10 percent to 13 percent higher in 2016 than the average premium for nongroup coverage in that same year under current law."

CHAPTER 12

1. "Recovery Act Allocates $1.1 Billion for Comparative Effectiveness Research," U.S. Department of Health and Human Services Press Release (undated); available at: http://www.hhs.gov/recovery/programs/os/cerbios.html [accessed May 2, 2010].

2. *The Patient Protection and Affordable Care Act*, HR 3590, 111th Cong., 2d sess., Section 6301; available at: http://frwebgate.access.gpo.gov/cgi-bin/getdoc.cgi?dbname=111_cong_bills&docid=f:h3590enr.txt.pdf [accessed June 9, 2010].

3. Matthew Hill report on NICE, BBC, Radio 4, first aired January 16, 2007; available at: www.bbc.co.uk/radio4/science/nice.shtml [accessed May 2, 2010].

4. "U-turn over asbestos cancer drug," BBC News, July 8, 2007; available at: http://news.bbc.co.uk/2/hi/health/6278118.stm [accessed April 30, 2010].

5. "Anger over arthritis drug refusal," BBC News, April 23, 2008; available at: http://news.bbc.co.uk/2/hi/health/7362989.stm [accessed June 9, 2010].

6. "Dismay over cancer drug guidance," BBC News, November 13, 2006; available at: http://news.bbc.co.uk/2/hi/health/6144274.stm [accessed May 2, 2010].

7. Jessica Best, "Families support Tory funds pledge," *South Wales Argus*, April 7, 2010; available at: http://www.southwalesargus.co.uk/news/7987028.Families_support_Tory_funds_pledge/ [accessed May 2, 2010].

8. Robert Winnett, "Andrew Dillon, Nice chief executive, knighted in New Year's honours," *UK Telegraph*, December 31, 2009; available at: http://www.telegraph.co.uk/health/healthnews/6912191/Andrew-

Dillon-Nice-chief-executive-knighted-in-New-Years-honours.html [accessed June 9, 2010].

9. "U.K.'s NICE says Bayer liver cancer drug too costly," Reuters, November 19, 2009; available at: http://www.reuters.com/article/idUSLI72915120091119 [accessed May 2, 2010].

10. Virginia Postrel, "My Drug Problem," *The Atlantic*, March 2009; available at: http://www.theatlantic.com/magazine/archive/2009/03/my-drug-problem/7279/ [accessed May 2, 2010].

11. "Screening for Breast Cancer," Recommendation Statement, Agency for Healthcare Research and Quality, December 2009; available at: http://www.ahrq.gov/clinic/uspstf/uspsbrca.htm [accessed May 2, 2010].

12. Editorial, "The Controversy Over Mammograms," *New York Times*, November 19, 2009; available at: http://www.nytimes.com/2009/11/20/opinion/20fri1.html [accessed April 28, 2010].

CHAPTER 13

1. "Cataract," Prevention of Blindness and Visual Impairment, World Health Organization, http://www.who.int/blindness/causes/priority/en/index1.html [accessed June 9, 2010].

2. Ed Silverman, "Spending On Prescription Drugs Rose 5.2% In 2009," *Pharmalot*, February 5, 2005; available at: http://www.pharmalot.com/2010/02/spending-on-prescription-drugs-rose-52-in-2009/ [accessed June 9, 2010].

3. *Health Care Costs: A Primer*, The Kaiser Family Foundation, March 2009; available at: http://www.kff.org/insurance/upload/7670_02.pdf [accessed June 9, 2010].

4. Robert Pear, "Spending Rise for Health Care and Prescription Drugs Slows," *New York Times*, January 5, 2009; available at: http://www.nytimes.com/2009/01/06/us/06healthcare.html [accessed June 9, 2010].

5. "U.S. Diabetes Rate Doubles In Last Decade," CBS News, October 30, 2008; available at: http://www.cbsnews.com/stories/2008/10/30/health/main4559539.shtml [accessed June 9, 2010].

6. "Diabetes," Chronic Disease Prevention and Health Promotion, Centers for Disease Control and Prevention, http://www.cdc.gov/

chronicdisease/resources/publications/AAG/ddt.htm [accessed June 9, 2010].

7. Miranda Hitti, "Heart Disease Kills Every 34 Seconds in U.S.," FOX News, December 27, 2004; available at: http://www.foxnews.com/story/0,2933,142436,00.html [accessed June 9, 2010].

8. Mark W. Stanton, "The High Concentration of U.S. Health Care Expenditures," *Research in Action*, Issue 19, U.S. Department of Health & Human Services, June 2006; available at: http://www.ahrq.gov/research/ria19/expendria.htm [accessed June 9, 2010].

9. "Just What the Doctor Ordered: Taking Medicines as Prescribed Can Improve Health and Lower Costs," PhRMA, March 2009; available at: http://www.phrma.org/files/attachments/Adherence.pdf [accessed June 9, 2010].

10. Baoping Shang and Dana P. Goldman, "Prescription Drug Coverage and Elderly Medicare Spending," *EconPapers*, No. 13358, 2007-9, http://econpapers.repec.org/paper/nbrnberwo/13358.htm [accessed June 9, 2010].

11. Frank Lichtenberg, "Benefits and Costs of New Drugs: Evidence from the Medical Expenditure PanelSurvey," *Health Affairs*, September/October 2001, 20(5):241–51.

12. "What goes into the cost of prescription drugs? . . . and other questions about your medicines," PhRMA, http://www.phrma.org/files/attachments/Cost_of_Prescription_Drugs.pdf [accessed June 9, 2010].

13. J. A. Dimasi and H. G. Grabowski, "The Cost of Biopharmaceutical R&D: Is Biotech Different?" *Managerial and Decision Economics* 28 (2007): 469–79.

CHAPTER 14

1. "Long-Term Care," Medicare.gov, http://www.medicare.gov/longtermcare/static/home.asp [accessed June 9, 2010].

2. William La Jeunesse, "Little-Known Health Care law Provision Is a Budget Buster, Critics Say," FOX News, March 26, 2010; available at: http://www.foxnews.com/politics/2010/03/26/little-known-long-termhealth-care-provision-budget-buster-say-critics/ [accessed June 9, 2010]; Richard S. Foster, "Estimated Financial Effects of the

'Patient Protection and Affordable Care Act as Amended,'" Balti-more: Centers for Medicare and Medicaid Services, April 22, 2010; available at: http://thehill.com/images/stories/whitepapers/pdf/oact%20memorandum%20on%20financial%20impact%20of%20ppaca%20as%20enacted.pdf [accessed June 15, 2010].

3. Letter from Douglas W. Elmendorf, Director Congressional Budget Office, to Honorable George Miller, November 25, 2009; available at: http://www.cbo.gov/ftpdocs/107xx/doc10769/CLASS_Additional_Information_Miller_letter.pdf [accessed June 9, 2010].

4. Richard S. Foster, "Estimated Financial Effects of the 'Patient Protection and Affordable Care Act as Amended,'" *op. cit.*

5. Letter from Douglas W. Elmendorf, Director of Congressional Budget Office, to Honorable George Miller, November 25, 2009, *op. cit.*

6. Richard S. Foster, "Estimated Financial Effects of the 'Patient Protection and Affordable Care Act as Amended,'" *op. cit.*

7. Ibid.

8. Ibid.

CHAPTER 15

1. Data available at: http://www.cbo.gov/ftpdocs/113xx/doc11379/Manager'sAmendmenttoReconciliationProposal.pdf

2. 2009 Annual Report of the Boards of Trustees of the Federal Hospital Insurance and Federal Supplementary Medical Insurance Trust Funds, http://www.cms.gov/ReportsTrustFunds/downloads/tr2009.pdf, p. 8 [accessed June 9, 2010].

3. Richard S. Foster, "Estimated Financial Effects of the 'Patient Protection and Affordable Care Act as Amended,'" *op. cit.*

4. "Medicare Fraud: A $60 Billion Crime," CBS News, October 25, 2009; available at: http://www.cbsnews.com/stories/2009/10/23/60minutes/main5414390.shtml [accessed June 9, 2010].

5. Richard S. Foster, "Estimated Financial Effects of the 'Patient Protection and Affordable Care Act as Amended,'" *op. cit.*

6. "Remarks by the President at the Annual Conference of the American Medical Association," The White House, Office of the Press Secretary, June 15, 2009; available at: http://www.whitehouse.gov/the_

press_office/Remarks-by-the-President-to-the-Annual-Conference-of-the-American-Medical-Association/ [accessed June 9, 2010].

7. Anne Tergesen, "Changes to Medicare Advantage," *Wall Street Journal*, May 9, 2010; available at: http://online.wsj.com/article/SB127336164057988979.html [accessed June 9, 2010].

8. Karl Rove, "Obama Targets Medicare Advantage," *Wall Street Journal*, August 26, 2009; available at: http://online.wsj.com/article/SB10001424052970203706604574374584177632694.html [accessed June 9, 2010].

9. "Medicare Advantage," Medicare Fact Sheet, The Henry J. Kaiser Family Foundation, November 2009; available at: http://www.kff.org/medicare/upload/2052-13.pdf [accessed June 9, 2010].

10. "Medicare Advantage: Private Health Plans in Medicare," CBO, June 28, 2007; available at: http://www.cbo.gov/ftpdocs/82xx/doc8268/06-28-Medicare_Advantage.pdf [accessed June 9, 2010].

11. Ibid.

12. *The Value of Private Sector Health Choices in Medicare* (Washington, D.C.: America's Health Insurance Plans, September 2004), 1–2.

13. "Comparison of Projected Enrollment in Medicare Advantage Plans and Subsidies for Extra Benefits Not Covered by Medicare Under Current Law and Under Reconciliation Legislation Combined with H.R. 3590 as Passed by the Senate," March 19, 2010; available at: http://www.cbo.gov/ftpdocs/113xx/doc11379/MAComparisons.pdf [accessed June 9, 2010].

14. "The Value of Extra Benefits Offered by Medicare Advantage Plans in 2006," *Medicare Issue Brief*; available at: http://www.kff.org/medicare/upload/7744.pdf [accessed June 9, 2010].

15. California Health care Foundation, *Snapshot: Financial Health of California Hospitals* (Oakland: California Health care Foundation, 2007), 12.

16. "Rethinking Comparative Effectiveness Research," http://www.ncbi.nlm.nih.gov/pmc/articles/PMC2799075/pdf/bth06_2p035.pdf [accessed June 9, 2010].

17. Jeff Jacoby, "Dangerous to our health," *Boston Globe*, June 16, 2010; available at: http://www.boston.com/bostonglobe/editorial_opin-

ion/oped/articles/2010/06/16/dangerous_to_our_health/ [accessed June 17, 2010].

18. Daniel Martin, "Betrayal of 20,000 cancer patients: Rationing body rejects ten drugs (allowed in Europe) that could have extended lives," *Daily Mail*, March 16, 2010; available at: http://www. dailymail.co.uk/health/article-1257944/NICE-rejects-cancer-drugs-extended-patients-lives.html [accessed June 9, 2010].

19. "Dr. Obama and Dr. Pelosi to America's Seniors: 'Take $523.5 Billion in Medicare Cuts; Don't Call Us in the Morning,'" Committee on Ways & Means Republicans, March 19, 2010; available at: http:// republicans.waysandmeans.house.gov/News/ DocumentSingle.aspx?DocumentID=177157 [accessed June 9, 2010].

20. "The Physicians' Perspective: Medical Practice in 2008," The Physicians' Foundation, http://www.mendocinohre.org/rhic/200811/PF_Report_Final.pdf [accessed June 9, 2010].

21. Jeffrey H. Anderson, "Obama's tax-funded propaganda campaign isn't swaying seniors on Obamacare," *Washington Examiner*, June 15, 2010; available at: http://www.washingtonexaminer.com/ opinion/blogs/beltway-confidential/obamas-tax-funded-propaganda-campaign-isnt-swaying-seniors-on-obamacare-96394709.html [accessed June 17, 2010]. See also, Perry Bacon Jr. and Michael D. Shear, "Obama town hall with seniors highlights $250 health-care rebate," *Washington Post*, June 8, 2010; available at: http://www.washingtonpost.com/wp-dyn/content/ article/2010/06/08/AR2010060800872.html [accessed June 17, 2010].

CHAPTER 16

1. Andrew Biggs, "Thinking about Healthcare Profitability," Critical Condition health blog, National Review Online, September 31, 2009; available at: http://www.nationalreview.com/critical-condition/ 48268/thinking-about-health-care-profitability/andrew-biggs [accessed June 10, 2010].

2. Glenn Thrush, "Nancy Pelosi: Insurers are 'immoral' villains," *Politico*, July 31, 2009; available at: http://www.politico.com/news/ stories/0709/25651.html [accessed June 10, 2010].

3.   "Top industries: Most profitable," Fortune 500, CNN.com, May 4, 2009; available at: http://money.cnn.com/magazines/fortune/fortune500/2009/performers/industries/profits/ [accessed June 10, 2010].

4.   "The Latest News in Health Reform," National Conference of State Legislatures, Updated June 8, 2010; available at: http://www.ncsl.org/?tabid=17639 [accessed June 10, 2010].

5.   Data available at: http://www.tradingday.com/basics/berkshire_hathaway.html [accessed June 10, 2010]; see also, Alex Crippen, "If Buffett Were President: Ask Warren Transcript—Part 3," CNBC.com, March 1, 2010; available at: http://www.cnbc.com/id/35643967/page/2/ [accessed June 10, 2010.

6.   "Minimum Loss Ratio Requirements," Hot Issues; available at: http://www.magnetmail.net/actions/email_web_version.cfm?recipient_id=180165729&message_id=677424&user_id=NAHU_2 [accessed June 10, 2010].

7.   Staff Report for Chairman Rockefeller, "Implementing Health Insurance Reform: New Medical Loss Ratio Information for Policymakers and Consumers," Committee on Commerce, Science, and Transportation, Office of Oversight and Investigations Majority Staff, April 15, 2010; available at: http://commerce.senate.gov/public/?a=Files.Serve&File_id=42805d51-b2a7-4cec-8a65-b13d61de9cbf [accessed June 10, 2010].

8.   "Minimum Loss Ratio Requirements," Hot Issues, *op. cit.*

9.   Ibid.

10. "State Mandatory Medical Loss Ratio (MLR) Requirements for Comprehensive, Major Medical Coverage: Summary of State Laws and Regulations (as of April 15, 2010)," National Association of Insurance Commissioners; available at: http://www.naic.org/documents/committees_lhatf_ahwg_100426_AHIP_MLR_Chart.pdf [accessed June 10, 2010]; see also, Nancy C. Turnbull and Nancy M. Kline, "INSURING THE HEALTHY OR INSURING THE SICK? THE DILEMMA OF REGULATING THE INDIVIDUAL HEALTH INSURANCE MARKET: FINDINGS FROM A STUDY OF SEVEN STATES," The Commonwealth Fund, February 2010; available at: http://www.commonwealthfund.org/~/media/Files/Publications/

Fund%20Report/2005/Feb/
Insuring%20the%20Healthy%20or%20Insuring%20the%20Sick%20
%20The%20Dilemma%20of%20Regulating%20the%20Individual%2
0Health%20Insurance/771_Turnbull_insuring_healthy_or_sick_
findings%20pdf.pdf [accessed June 10, 2010].

11. Individual Health Insurance 2009, AHIP, Center for Policy and
Research, October 2009; available at: http://www.ahipresearch.org/
pdfs/2009IndividualMarketSurveyFinalReport.pdf [accessed June
10, 2010].

12. Susan Heavey, "Health Insurers Shifting Costs Ahead of Law:
Report," ABC News, April 15, 2010; available at: http://
abcnews.go.com/Politics/wireStory?id=10385282 [accessed June 10,
2010].

13. "UPDATE: Health Insurers Debate Medical-Cost Meaning In
Reform," *Wall Street Journal*, April 13, 2010; available at: http://
online.wsj.com/article/BT-CO-20100413-711946.html [accessed
June 10, 2010].

14. David S. Hilzenrath, "Insurers, commissioners hammer out details
of health-care reform," *Washington Post*, May 13, 2010; available at:
http://www.washingtonpost.com/wp-dyn/content/article/2010/
05/13/AR2010051302024.html?wpisrc=nl_wonk [accessed June 10,
2010].

15. "Critical Issues in Health Reform, Minimum Loss Ratios," American
Academy of Actuaries, July 2009; available at: http://www.
actuary.org/pdf/health/loss_july09.pdf [accessed June 10, 2010].

CHAPTER 17

1. Jones Day Law Firm, "Impact of health care reform legislation on
employer-sponsored group health plans," Section II. B,
Lexology.com; available at: http://www.lexology.com/library/
detail.aspx?g=fc532e9e-606c-496f-a053-c190c87e65f1 [accessed
May 9, 2010].

2. Ibid., Section III. E. 5.

3. Ibid.

4. "The End of HSAs," *Wall Street Journal*, November 23, 2009; available at: http://online.wsj.com/article/

SB10001424052748704204304574545814221561286.html [accessed May 9, 2010].

5. Ron Bachman, "Congress Declares War on HSAs," National Center for PolicyAnalysis online, March 5, 2010; available at: http://www.ncpa.org/pub/ba698 [accessed May 9, 2010].

6. Alex Tabarrok, "Consumer Driven Health Plans," Marginal Revolution Economics Blog, posted August 12, 2009; available at: http://www.marginalrevolution.com/marginalrevolution/2009/08/consumer-drive-health-care-plans.html [accessed May 9, 2010].

7. Jones Day Law Firm, "Impact of health care reform legislation on employer-sponsored group health plans," Section III. F. 2, *op. cit.*

8. Ron Bachman, "Congress Declares War on HSAs," *op. cit.*

9. Roy Ramthun, "Dr. HSA," Medical Banking Policy Research, March 2010; available at: http://www.mbproject.org/column-harris.php [accessed June 10, 2010].

10. Julie Appleby, "Insurance Industry Faces Tough Scrutiny From Federal Watchdogs," *Kaiser Health News*, June 1, 2010; available at: http://www.kaiserhealthnews.org/Stories/2010/June/01/Insurance-Industry-Faces-Tough-Scrutiny-From-Federal-Watchdogs.aspx [accessed June 17, 2010].

11. Linda Gorman, "If you like your plan you can keep it...er...hmm...so long as I also like it," John Goodman's Health Policy Blog, posted July 28, 2009; available at: http://www.john-goodmanblog.com/if-you-like-your-plan-you-can-keep-iterhmmso-long-as-i-also-like-it/ [accessed June 10, 2010].

12. Jennifer Haberkorn, "New regs strict with 'grandfathers,'" *Politico*, June 15, 2010; available at: http://www.politico.com/news/stories/0610/38523.html [accessed June 17, 2010].

13. Information available at: http://www.federalregister.gov/OFRUpload/OFRData/2010-14488_PI.pdf.

14. Ibid., 76

15. Ibid., 81–82

16. Ibid, 54

17. Ibid.

CHAPTER 18

1. Press Release, "2010 Easter Egg Roll," The White House; available at: http://www.whitehouse.gov/easterEggRoll [accessed June 10, 2010].

2. Michael Gerson, "With health-care reform, it's nag, nag, nag," *Washington Post*, April 23, 2010; available at: http://www.washingtonpost.com/wp-dyn/content/article/2010/04/22/AR2010042204210.html [accessed June 10, 2010].

3. Jacob Sullum, "You Can Show a Fat Bastard Calories, But You Can't Make Him Count," *Reason*, October 7, 2009; available at: http://reason.com/blog/2009/10/07/you-can-show-a-fat-bastard-cal [accessed June 10, 2010].

4. Ibid.

5. Ibid.

6. Roni Caryn Rabin, "How Posted Calories Affect Food Orders," *New York Times*, November 2, 2009; available at: http://www.nytimes.com/2009/11/03/health/03nutrition.html [accessed June 10, 2010].

7. News Release, "National Restaurant Association Outlines Concerns With Passage of Health Care Bill In U.S. House," National Restaurant Association, March 21, 2010; available at: http://www.restaurant.org/pressroom/pressrelease/?ID=1909 [accessed June 10, 2010].

8. Sarah Rubenstein, "McDonald's CEO Queasy Over Restaurant Calorie Counts," *Wall Street Journal*, May 19, 2008; available at: http://blogs.wsj.com/health/2008/05/19/mcdonalds-ceo-queasy-over-restaurant-calorie-counts/ [accessed June 10, 2010].

9. Focus on Health Reform, "Summary of Coverage Provisions in the Patient Protection and Affordable Care Act," The Henry J. Kaiser Family Foundation, updated April 28, 2010; available at: http://www.kff.org/healthreform/upload/8023-R.pdf [accessed June 10, 2010].

10. W. Kip Viscusi, *Smoking: Making the Risky Decision* (New York: Oxford University Press, 1992), 77.

11. "Health Reform Implementation Timeline," The Henry J. Kaiser Family Foundation; available at: http://www.kff.org/healthreform/8060.cfm [accessed June 10, 2010].

12. Kristin Voigt and Harald Schmidt, "Wellness Programs: A Threat to Fairness and Affordable Care," The Hastings Center; see also, Roni Caryn Rabin, "Could Health Overhaul Incentives Hurt Someone?" *New York Times*, April 12, 2010; available at: http://www.nytimes.com/2010/04/13/health/13land.html [accessed June 10, 2010].

13. Ibid.

14. "Hewitt Survey Shows Growing Interest Among U.S. Employers to Penalize Workers for Unhealthy Behaviors," March 17, 2010; available at: http://www.hewittassociates.com/Intl/NA/en-US/AboutHewitt/Newsroom/PressReleaseDetail.aspx?cid=8256 [accessed June 10, 2010].

15. Ibid.

16. "Remarks of Senator Barack Obama," *New York Times*, May 29, 2007; available at: http://www.nytimes.com/2007/05/29/us/politics/28text-obama.html [accessed June 10, 2010].

17. Nancy Pelosi and Steny Hoyer, "'Un-American' attacks can't derail health care debate," *USA Today*, August 10, 2009; available at: http://blogs.usatoday.com/oped/2009/08/unamerican-attacks-cant-derail-health-care-debate-.html [accessed June 10, 2010].

18. "Prevention and Wellness" CBO Director's Blog, posted August 9, 2009; available at: http://cboblog.cbo.gov/?p=345 [accessed June 10, 2010].

19. Memo, Richard S. Foster, "Estimated Financial Effects of the 'Patient Protection and Affordable Care Act' as Amended," Centers for Medicare and Medicaid Services, April 22, 2010; available at: http://graphics8.nytimes.com/packages/pdf/health/oactmemo1.pdf [accessed June 10, 2010].

20. Matt Miller, "Why prevention won't cure health care," *Fortune*, July 9, 2009; available at: http://money.cnn.com/2009/07/09/news/economy/prevention_wont_save_health care.fortune/index.htm [accessed June 10, 2010].

21. Joshua T. Cohen, Ph.D., Peter J. Neumann, Sc.D., and Milton C. Weinstein, Ph.D., "Does Preventive Care Save Money? Health Economics and the Presidential Candidates," *New England Journal of*

Medicine, February 14, 2008; available at: http://content.nejm.org/cgi/content/full/358/7/661[accessed June 10, 2010].

22. Luc Bonneux, "Preventing fatal diseases increases healthcare cost: cause elimination lifetable approach," *British Medical Journal* online, January 3, 1998; available at: http://www.bmj.com/cgi/content/abstract/316/7124/26 [accessed June 10, 2010].

23. Report, "Public Finance Balance of Smoking in Czech Republic," Arthur D. Little Internation, Inc. commissioned by Philip Morris CI, November 28, 2000; available at: http://www.tobaccofreekids.org/reports/philipmorris/pmczechstudy.pdf [accessed June 10, 2010].

24. Associated Press, "Study: Fat People Cheaper to Treat," *USA Today*, February 5, 2008; available at: http://www.usatoday.com/news/health/2008-02-05-obese-cost_N.htm [accessed June 10, 2010], citing this paper: http://medicine.plosjournals.org/perlserv/?request=get-document&doi=10.1371/journal.pmed.0050029 [accessed June 10, 2010].

25. van Baal PHM, Polder JJ, de Wit GA, Hoogenveen RT, Feenstra TL, et al., "Lifetime Medical Costs of Obesity: Prevention No Cure for Increasing Health Expenditure," *PloS Medicine*, 5(2), 2009; available at: http://www.plosmedicine.org/article/info:doi/10.1371/journal.pmed.0050029 [accessed June 10, 2010].

CHAPTER 19

1. Barack Obama, Remarks in Dover, New Hampshire, September 12, 2008; available at: http://www.presidency.ucsb.edu/ws/index.php?pid=78612 [accessed June 10, 2010].

2. Ibid.

3. Paul Ryan, "Fix Health Reform, Then Repeal It," *New York Times*, March 25, 2010; available at: http://www.nytimes.com/2010/03/26/opinion/26ryan.html [accessed June 10, 2010].

4. "Taxes and Small Business Job Creation," Statement of Chris Edwards, Director of Tax Policy Studies, Cato Institute, before the Committee on Finance, United States Senate, February 23, 2010; available at: http://www.cato.org/testimony/ct-ce-20100223.htmla [accessed June 15, 2010].

5. Annie Baxter, "Excise Tax Has Local Medical Device Makers Concerned," Minnesota Public Radio, March 29, 2010; available at: http://minnesota.publicradio.org/display/web/2010/03/29/medical-excise-tax/ [accessed June 10, 2010].

6. Small Biz Stats & Trends, Score, http://www.score.org/small_biz_stats.html [accessed June 10, 2010].

7. Compound Interest Calculator, http://www.moneychimp.com/calculator/compound_interest_calculator.htm.

8. John K. Higgins, "Health Insurance CRM, Part 1: Shifting Into Catch-Up Mode," *CRM Buyer*, November 19, 2009; available at: http://www.crmbuyer.com/story/68690.html [accessed June 10, 2010].

9. Peter Grier, "Health care reform bill 101: Who will pay for reform?" *Christian Science Monitor*, March 21, 2010; available at: http://www.csmonitor.com/USA/Politics/2010/0321/Health-care-reform-bill-101-Who-will-pay-for-reform [accessed June 10, 2010].

10. Tax Policy Center, Quick Facts: Alternative Minimum Tax (AMT), http://www.taxpolicycenter.org/taxtopics/quick_amt.cfm [accessed June 10, 2010].

11. "Cumulative Changes in Health Insurance Premiums, Inflation, and Workers' Earnings, 1999-2000," Kaiser Fast Facts, http://facts.kff.org/chart.aspx?ch=707 [accessed June 10, 2010].

12. "Potential Impact of Health Reform on the Cost of Private Health Insurance Coverage," Pricewaterhouse Coopers, October 2009; available at: http://www.americanhealthsolution.org/assets/Reform-Resources/AHIP-Reform-Resources/PWC-Report-on-Costs-Final.pdf [accessed June 10, 2010].

13. Ibid.

14. Health Care Reform Premium Impact in Virginia—DECEMBER 2009 ADDENDUM, http://wellpoint.com/pdf/December_2009_Analysis_Virginia_Update.pdf [accessed June 10, 2010].

15. Health Care Reform Premium Impact in Kentucky—DECEMBER 2009 ADDENDUM, http://wellpoint.com/pdf/December_2009_Analysis_Kentucky_Update.pdf [accessed June 10, 2010].

CHAPTER 20

1. Shailagh Murray and Lori Montgomery, "House passes health-care reform bill without Republican votes," *Washington Post*, March 22, 2010; available at: http://www.washingtonpost.com/wp-dyn/content/article/2010/03/21/AR2010032100943.html [accessed June 15, 2010].

2. "Obama Quotes Lincoln To House Dems: 'I Am Bound To Be True,'" *Huffington Post*, March 21, 2010; available at: http://www.huffingtonpost.com/2010/03/20/obama-quotes-lincoln-to-h_n_507124.html [accessed June 15, 2010].

3. Philip Klein, "CBO Adds $115 Billion to ObamaCare Cost Estimate," *American Spectator*, May 11, 2010; available at: http://spectator.org/blog/2010/05/11/cbo-adds-115-billion-to-obamac [accessed June 15, 2010].

4. United States Senate Budget Committee, Senator Gregg's Senate Floor Remarks on the True Cost of Democrats' Senate Health Care Reform Bill, November 21, 2009; available at: http://budget.senate.gov/republican/pressarchive/2009-11-21Floor.pdf [accessed June 15, 2010].

5. Data available at: http://budget.senate.gov/republican/pressarchive/2009/2009-11-19Health careFactSheet.pdf

6. Michael Cannon, "Do the Math—Obamacare Would Increase Deficits by $59 Billion," FOX News, March 20, 2010; available at: http://www.foxnews.com/opinion/2010/03/20/michael-f-cannon-cato-cbo-health-care-reform-democrats-false/ [accessed June 15, 2010].

7. Richard S. Foster, Memorandum, "Estimated Financial Effects of the 'Patient Protection and Affordable Care Act' as Amended," Centers for Medicare and Medicaid Services, April 22, 2010; available at: http://www.politico.com/static/PPM130_oact_memorandum_on_financial_impact_of_ppaca_as_enacted.html [accessed June 17, 2010].

8. Julian Pecquet, "White House defends healthcare law as reducing budget deficit," *The Hill*, June 2, 2010; available at: http://thehill.com/homenews/news/101103-white-house-defends-healthcare-law-as-reducing-budget-deficit [accessed June 17, 2010].

9.   Douglas Holtz-Eakin and Cameron Smith, "Labor Markets and Health Care Reform: New Results," American Action Forum, May 2010; available at: http://americanactionforum.org/files/LaborMkt-sHCRAAF5-27-10_0.pdf [accessed June 17, 2010].

10.   Douglas W. Elmendorf, Director Congressional Budget Office, letter to the Honorable Paul Ryan, March 19, 2010; available at: http://www.cbo.gov/ftpdocs/113xx/doc11376/RyanLtrhr4872.pdf [accessed June 15, 2010].

11.   Ibid.

12.   Ibid.

13.   Sam Brownback, Memorandum, "Are Health Care Reform Cost Estimates Reliable?" Joint Economic Committe, July 31, 2009; available at: http://jec.senate.gov/republicans/public/?a=files.serve&File_id=5802c84c-2821-4ab3-bacb-793f3ae2e036 [accessed June 17, 2010].

14.   *Economic Report of the President*, transmitted to the Congress February 2010; available at: http://www.gpoaccess.gov/eop/2010/2010_erp.pdf, p. 423 [accessed June 15, 2010].

15.   Ibid., 424.

16.   Ibid., 426.

CHAPTER 21

1.   Ashley Halsey III, "Primary-Care Doctor Shortage May Undermine Reform Efforts," *Washington Post*, June 20, 2009; available at: http://www.washingtonpost.com/wp-dyn/content/article/2009/06/19/AR2009061903583.html [accessed June 15, 2010].

2.   "Statistics Highlight The Looming Doctor Shortage," *Medical News Today*, August 19, 2009; available at: http://www.medicalnewstoday.com/articles/161128.php [accessed June 15, 2010].

3.   2009 Survey of Physician Appointment Wait Times, Merritt Hawkins & Associates, http://www.merritthawkins.com/pdf/mha2009waittimesurvey.pdf [accessed June 15, 2010].

4.   Ashley Halsey III, "Primary-Care Doctor Shortage May Undermine Reform Efforts," *op. cit.*

5.   Ibid.

6. Parija B. Kavilanz, "Rx for money woes: Doctors quit medicine," CNN-Money.com, September 30, 2009; available at: http://money.cnn.com/2009/09/14/news/economy/health_care_doctors_quitting/index.htm?postversion=2009091404 [accessed June 15, 2010].

7. Terry Jones, "45% Of Doctors Would Consider Quitting If Congress Passes Health Care Overhaul," Investors.com, September 15, 2009; available at: http://www.investors.com/newsandanalysis/article.aspx?id=506199 [accessed June 15, 2010].

8. David Hogberg, "ObamaCare Rules For Paying Doctors Might Spur Exodus," Investors.com, March 30, 2010; available at: http://www.investors.com/NewsAndAnalysis/Article.aspx?id=528916 [accessed June 15, 2010].

9. Gautham Nagesh, "Arizona doctor says Obamacare will force him to close shop," The Daily Caller, April 14, 2010; available at: http://dailycaller.com/2010/04/14/arizona-doctor-says-obamacare-will-force-him-to-close-shop/ [accessed June 15, 2010].

10. David Hogberg, "ObamaCare Rules For Paying Doctors Might Spur Exodus," *op. cit.*

11. Ibid.

12. Deval L. Patrick and Timothy P. Murray, "Governor Patrick Announces $21.2 Billion Medicaid Waiver Agreement," Governor Deval Patrick official website, September 30, 2008; available at: http://www.mass.gov/?pageID=gov3pressrelease&L=1&L0=Home&sid=Agov3&b=pressrelease&f=093008_waiver&csid=Agov3 [accessed June 15, 2010].

13. Andrea Seabrook, "Mass. Health Care Reform Reveals Doctor Shortage," NPR, *All Things Considered*, November 30, 2008; transcript available at: http://www.npr.org/templates/transcript/transcript.php?storyId=97620520 [accessed June 15, 2010].

14. Ibid.

CHAPTER 23

1. *Medicare Catastrophic Coverage Act of 1988*, HR 2470, 100th Cong., 1987–1988; available at: http://thomas.loc.gov/cgi-bin/bdquery/z?d100:HR02470:@@@L&summ2=m&|TOM:/bss/d100query.html [accessed June 10, 2010].

2.   Karen Tumulty and Kate Pickert, with Alice Park, "What Does It Do
      to Medicare?" *Time*, March 25, 2010; available at: http://www.
      time.com/time/specials/packages/article/0,28804,1975068_
      1975012_1975001,00.html, p. 3 of 18 [accessed June 10, 2010].

3.   Larry Pratt, "GOA Members Help another Senator 'See the Light,'"
      Gun Owners of America, 2010; available at: http://gunowners.org/
      nws0007.htm [accessed June 10, 2010].

4.   "Medicare Catastrophic Coverage Act," http://www.answers.com/
      topic/medicare-catastrophic-coverage-act [accessed June 15, 2010].

5.   "Health Care Law," Rasmussen Reports, June 7, 2010; available at:
      http://www.rasmussenreports.com/public_content/politics/
      current_events/healthcare/march_2010/health_care_law [accessed
      June 10, 2010].

6.   Philip Klein, "GOP's Health Care Strategy Is Short-Sighted," *Ameri-
      can Spectator*, October 2, 2009; available at: http://spectator.org/
      archives/2009/10/02/gops-health-care-strategy-is-s [accessed June
      10, 2010].

7.   "January 2010 Census Shows 10 Million People Covered by HSA/
      High-Deductible Health Plans," AHIP Center for Policy and
      Research, May 2010; available at: http://www.ahipresearch.org/
      pdfs/HSA2010.pdf [accessed June 10, 2010].

8.   "Health Care Law Changes HSA Spending," *CVN News*, May 17,
      2010; available at: http://www.coosavalleynews.com/np85377.htm
      [accessed June 10, 2010].

9.   Rich Kahler, "KAHLER: Begin planning now for higher health care
      costs, taxes," *Rapid City Journal*, May 21, 2010; available at: http://
      www.rapidcityjournal.com/business/article_c66c8f36-6467-11df-
      953e-001cc4c03286.html [accessed June 10, 2010].

10.   Sally C. Pipes, "Six Fixes For Lowering Healthcare Costs," County-
      PressOnline.com, December 23, 2008; available at: http://www.
      pacificresearch.org/docLib/20090102_20081223_County_Press_
      PA.pdf [accessed June 10, 2010].

11.   Ibid.

12.   Ibid.

13.   Lawrence J. McQuillan, "CBO Underestimates Benefits of Malprac-
      tice Reform," *Wall Street Journal*, October 23, 2009; available at:

http://online.wsj.com/article/SB10001424052748703573604574491-690229571588.html [accessed June 10, 2010].

14. Sally C. Pipes, *The Top Ten Myths of American Health Care, op. cit.*

15. Lawrence J. McQuillan, Hovannes Abramyan, and Anthony P. Archie, with Jeffrey A. Johnson and Anna Erokhina, *Jackpot Justice: The True Cost of America's Tort System* (Pacific Research Institute, 2007); available at: http://www.pacificresearch.org/docLib/20070327_Jackpot_Justice.pdf [accessed June 10, 2010].

16. Eric Torbenson and Jason Roberson, "Tort Reform," *Dallas Morning News*, June 17, 2007; available at: http://www.dallasnews.com/sharedcontent/dws/bus/stories/DN-medmal_17bus.ART0.State.Edition2.43983f4.html [accessed June 10, 2010].

17. Lawrence J. McQuillan, et al., *Jackpot Justice: The True Cost of America's Tort System, op. cit.*

18. Ibid.

INDEX

ABOUT THE AUTHOR

SALLY C. PIPES

Sally C. Pipes is president and chief executive officer of the Pacific Research Institute, and is a renowned expert on health care and economic issues. She has been seen on NBC's *Nightly News with Brian Williams* and *The Today Show,* Fox News' *The Glenn Beck Show* and *The O'Reilly Factor,* ABC's *20/20* with John Stossel, CNN's *Lou Dobbs Show,* and many other TV and radio shows. She writes regular columns for the *Examiner* newspapers, *Chief Executive,* and *Investor's Business Daily,* and her opinion pieces have appeared in many publications, including *The New York Times*, *The Wall Street Journal*, and *The Washington Post*. She is a member of the Mont Pelerin Society, an international society of free-market economists and philosophers. Pipes, a former Canadian, knows too much about Canada's government-run health care system and became an American citizen in 2006. She lives in California, dividing her time between San Francisco, Sacramento, and Claremont, with her husband, Professor Charles Kesler.